P9-EES-963

WE'VE ALL
GOT
SCARS

WE'VE ALL GOT SCARS

What Boys and Girls
Learn in Elementary School

RAPHAELA BEST

INDIANA UNIVERSITY PRESS
BLOOMINGTON

To the children, the teachers, and the principal
of Pine Hill, from whom I learned so much.

Copyright © 1983 by Raphaela Best

All rights reserved

No part of this book may be reproduced or utilized in any form
or by any means, electronic or mechanical, including photocopying
and recording, or by any information storage and retrieval system,
without permission in writing from the publisher. The Association
of American University Presses' Resolution on Permissions constitutes
the only exception to this prohibition.

Manufactured in the United States of America

Library of Congress Cataloging in Publication Data

Best, Raphaela, 1925–
    We've all got scars.

    1. Interaction analysis in education.   2. Child
development.   3. Sex differences in education.
4. School environment.   5. Age groups.   I. Title.
LB1033.B48   1983   370.19'345   82-49198
ISBN 0-253-36420-5
1 2 3 4 5 87 86 85 84 83

LB
1033
S48
. 1983

CONTENTS

Foreword

The mid-seventies were a time of intellectual ferment in the feminist movement. A great wave of scholarship burst forth from libraries, archives, and computers. A whole new vision of what I have come to call the female world was spreading. It was dawning on more and more students of the current scene that from kindergarten on, a great deal that was being taught about women did not reflect the way women really were. There was an explosion of books, polemics, and discussions on what it was that produced the image of women. School textbooks and adult media were scrutinized in detail to show, step by step, how little children were inducted into their adult roles. Consciousness was being raised. This book belongs to the genre. It complements the solid tomes with their pages of tables and graphs with vignettes of the actual children being socialized into anachronistic attitudes and roles. Instead of the laboratory and statistical studies it gives us the boys and girls themselves. Those of us who write the abstract treatises can only be grateful to Ms. Best for showing us our theories in the actual context of real boys and girls. She adds also to our knowledge of the "third curriculum" the children create and teach one another, a thought-provoking contribution to the ongoing discussion of "sex education," suggesting that if you teach youngsters to talk to one another they can learn to know one another as friends rather than as sparring partners.

Ms. Best's story of peer-group influence on boys' academic achievement reads like a public-health warning: the macho role that the male world imposes on small boys by way of their peers is dangerous to their—emotional—health. It imposes stresses on them that six- to eight-year-old boys are not ready for. Nor, as we are now learning in the 1980s, are many adult males themselves ready for them.

Every reader of this book will retain a favorite vignette from the stories it tells of boys and girls as they move from kindergarten to junior high school in a time—the middle seventies—when questions about the most appropriate sex roles for this day and age are producing great social turmoil. Mine include: the little boy being registered for kindergarten who announced to the interviewer that he was exceptionally bright while the little girl called attention to her pretty dress; the second-grade boys fighting it out among themselves to see who could be boss as they lined up to watch the long-awaited hatching of chicks, thus missing the whole show while the girls watched it all serenely at close range; Tracey asking the boys if she could be a boy and, since she could pass all the tests, gaining their permission; the terrified third-grade girl who thought she might be pregnant; Jonathan, who won a class election on the platform "Jonathan fights for women's rights"; wheeler-dealer Chad explaining how he "fake-liked" Billy, the bully-boy; Jonathan, who did not like to fight, advising another boy that although fighting was a necessary proof of manhood there were ways of simulating it; Laura, who thanked Sonya for letting her win a race; and Elaine, who spoke of housework and motherhood as a "lot of pain."

It is equally absorbing to watch these children as a group, as well as individually, as they work their way through the three curricula Ms. Best distinguished—the academic curriculum, the sex-role curriculum, and the self-devised sex-education curriculum—the last of which is not yet well understood. To watch how, for example, one particular issue of the *National Geographic* becomes dog-eared with use on the basis of messages spread by word-of-mouth. How lack of an adequate vocabulary impedes the children's understanding of their own feelings. The boys and girls were, for example, greatly handicapped in their relationships by the limited vocabulary they had at their disposal for dealing with them. The verbal gamut ranged from "hate" to "not like" to "like" to "love." Hate was a fairly simple emotion. It might or might not have a sexual connotation. Sometimes it was a necessary denial of love. Thus, if a girl was accused of loving a boy, she could not merely say that she did not love him; she had to say she hated him. "Not liking" was a possible softer form of hate. But the two most equivocal terms were "like" and "love." Clarification became one of the earliest chores that had to be undertaken. The discussion of this curriculum will be of interest to both parents and teachers.

Ms. Best felt that the traditional roles the children were being socialized into were not suitable for the world they were going to live in as adults. She considered it important to have them challenge the stereotypes with reality. She wanted to make it possible for members of both sexes to deal with one another as friends. There were some who had misguided fears that she would reverse the sex stereotypes, turning boys into namby-pamby sissies and girls into tough tomboys. Actually the idea was not, for example, to dampen the boys' drive to win but only to show that playing could be fun no matter what the score.

The children we meet in this book, both individually and in groups, belong to a cohort that is going to leave a unique imprint on our society as, of course, every cohort does. They are now—fall of 1982—about to enter their last year of high school. They were born in the mid-sixties and all the alarms of the decade of the late sixties to the late seventies will seem of only historical interest to them. Less and less protected by the sheltering environment, they will graduate in 1983 into a world whose lineaments neither we nor they can yet trace. As I read about their childhood development I feel reassured. They seem to me to be well prepared. I think the world will be safe in their hands.

This book is the result of four years of intensive observation. When in the spring of 1972, Ms. Best, a reading specialist in a nearby school system, told me she believed on the basis of many years of experience that reading achievement among boys in elementary school was associated with their peer relationships, her evidence seemed interesting. I told her to research the question. She did. The following fall she began a program of daily, almost minute-by-minute observation of primary-age children in a local school. As the year progressed it became clear that she was accumulating a cache of data almost unprecedented in the research literature, not only with respect to her original problem—the relationship between peer group membership or nonmembership and reading ability among boys—but also a great deal more in an area—peers in interaction—that one distinguished scholar, Marian Radke Yarrow, has called "frontier research." She was seeing processes at work that escape the standard research approaches, approaches that yield yards of computer printouts but leave shrouded the essential human core within them. Before-and-after tables are still-frames; the process behind them is missing. Ms. Best was seeing sociological processes in action, as a biologist might watch biological processes under a microscope. The result is one of the few research studies of schools in which the emphasis is on the children themselves, not on the teachers. And they come through as real and alive, busy with their own complex world and not as, in effect, merely "dependent variables."

Although written in nontechnical language, the book should find appreciative readers among other professionals as well as among teachers. Students of child development will be grateful for its investigation of "peer-group interactions among six-, seven-, and eight-year-olds," an area that, according to Willard Hartup, has "not been thoroughly explored." The book also deals with "peer influence and group behavior among girls," about which, Hartup tells us, "our knowledge is appallingly weak." As a sociologist I was fascinated by the account of the processes of group formation among the boys in the second and third grades, and I think my fellow sociologists will be equally interested. It goes without saying that social psychologists will find the examples of how the macho pattern is imposed on boys supportive of their own work; they may be surprised to find how little the girls conform to the usual picture of a passive, dependent child, yet how well they conform to other norms for their gender roles. But most of all, this book should appeal to anyone who is interested in children and how they grow, and in the schools where they do so much of their growing.

Parents, finally, will, I think, learn a lot from these children. They educate us in spite of ourselves. They teach us how we look to them, how many chances we miss to make ourselves felt. We become aware that we are being watched, judged, graded. And that we may not be transmitting what we think we are.

JESSIE BERNARD

INTRODUCTION

From 1973 to 1977, I observed a group of children at Pine Hill,* an elementary school in one of the most affluent counties in the United States, as they organized their own intense, seething little world with its own frontiers, its own struggles, its own winners and losers. It was a world invisible to outsiders, not apparent to the casual observer, but, as I soon learned, one with a system of rewards and punishments powerful enough to affect the progress of boys—but not of girls—in learning to read. I was at Pine Hill to find out why.

As a reading specialist, I was aware of the high boy-girl ratio of reading disability. Research shows that in some schools reading disabilities are four times more frequent among boys than among girls, in other schools nine times more frequent, and in still others as much as twenty-five times more frequent.[1] The fact that nearly a million teenage youngsters, primarily boys, cannot read at even the level of a fourth-grader has elicited a wide variety of explanations, including: environmental factors; the learning process and conditions affecting it; individual developmental factors; physical factors (the "hygiene of reading" approach deals with the ease of seeing with the human eye); and pedagogical factors. Yet there were children with whom I had worked who had suffered none of the kinds of disabilities or disadvantages associated with the various factors and still did not learn to read; and there were some who, though they suffered from one or more, did nevertheless learn to read.

It was this paradox that challenged me more and more after years of experience in schools. Little by little it occurred to me that something in the peer-group environment was involved in a large number of the reading disabilities I was dealing with, and it was this hunch—too unformulated as yet to qualify as a hypothesis—that led me to take a year to study just what, if anything, there was in the male peer-group environment that influenced learning to read.

This project required a considerable commitment of time and energy. Research short-cuts like standardized instruments were not

*To avoid embarrassment for the children introduced in this book, who are now nearing high-school graduation, all names have been changed. The name of the school, located in the Central Atlantic region of the United States, has also been changed.

1

feasible. Because the primary-age children were only six, seven, and eight years old when the study began, they could not take paper and pencil tests. When tests were devised that required first-graders to respond by circling a smiling face or a frowning face, the children told adults only what they thought adults wanted to hear. Nor, as I knew from many years of experience, was it adequate for my purposes to be only a sidelines observer taking copious notes, for that had a dampening effect on students and teachers alike. Instead, I became a participant-observer. That meant working with children on instructional projects, playing games with them in the classroom and on the playground, eating lunch with them—perhaps the most intimate time of the day—and being a friend when they needed one. Although some researchers have dismissed this method as impractical, I knew of no other way to obtain the information on the children's peers groups, friendships, and gender-role socialization patterns needed to answer the questions posed by this study. So, with no illusions about the difficulties, I undertook the "impractical" way of "following the children . . . around."[2]

Although I was not a classroom teacher and had no influence over the homework the children were given or the grades they received, they viewed me as a member of the school establishment because I was an adult within the school. I was able to mitigate punishments and facilitate rewards. Thus, when the boys in the third grade formed the exclusively male Tent Club, I was invited to join because, although a woman, I was useful to them. They had guessed, correctly, that I would use any influence I had on their behalf. Though I was part of the establishment, the children knew I was on their side.

In the base year, regrettably, all of the children in the study were white, so that race as a variable is not involved here. However, Pine Hill's population came from a fairly wide class spectrum that included so-called Title I children, that is, children poor enough to be entitled to free lunches at that time. As a result of boundary changes, the black children had been assigned to a newly opened school, which they attended with children from the wealthier residential areas. The findings from Pine Hill, therefore, though not immediately applicable to black children, are nevertheless peripherally relevant. The black child who is excluded from his peer group may be subject to the same learning disadvantage as that to be discussed in this study. The same may be true for excluded minorities of all kinds.

After the first year, Pine Hill was once again racially balanced. In fact, during the last three years of the study, the school became known as a little United Nations, as children from many ethnic and racial backgrounds—Vietnamese, Burmese, Thai, East Indian, Nigerian, Pakastani, and Colombian, to name a few—enrolled there. That Pine Hill was able to manage this diversity and maintain the lowest vandalism rate in a high-risk part of the county (during one school year not a single act of vandalism occurred, and in another the replacement of an outside light broken by children playing ball after school hours was the only major repair the school system had to make) was in part attributable to the policies and practices of the school principal, Dr. "G."

A firm believer in the community school concept, Dr. "G." made parents welcome in the school and eased staff fears about parental involvement in the classroom. He maintained an open-door policy for children, teachers, and parents alike. He was never too busy to listen, advise, counsel, or extend a few words of praise for work well done. A walk through the school by the principal meant that heads would be patted, shoestrings tied for very young children, questions asked about schoolwork, or, in the case of a troubled child, inquiries made about what he could do to help. He was even known to cleanse and bandage elbows and knees bloodied on the playground. Dr. "G." was, in short, the ideal school administrator. He knew that what he did and said were important factors in how students and staff felt and behaved.

It was a school maxim that "every teacher is the teacher of every child." This philosophy created a family ambience within the school. Thus, when Ronnie's mother enrolled him in third grade at Pine Hill she said, "We moved to this community because we heard that Pine Hill has loving teachers." The innovations that took place in the last three years of this study and the results reported in chapters 10–12 might have been quite different in another school environment.

This study, however, puts the teacher into the background and focuses on the children themselves. Adults are by design kept conspicuously inconspicuous. They could not, of course, be wholly ignored. They were a part of the children's world, and, especially in the first grade, an extremely important part. But they are dealt with here only as part of the children's environment, not as themselves players of leading roles in the drama of the classroom and playground. The objective was to concentrate on the busy, complex, effervescent world the children lived and worked in—the world they created for themselves—and its effect on their learning.

Peer influences among school-age children have been neglected by researchers because of the traditionally strong emphasis on the role of the mother and the teacher in child development, but there is growing evidence that the influence of peers may be equally important to that of parents, if not more so. Indeed, in terms of species history, Lewis and Rosenblum tell us, the more usual pattern of child-rearing has probably involved socialization more by peers, including siblings, than by adults.

> Current research [in our society] tends to support adult-child models but observation of other cultures suggests that alternative models of rearing are possible and have consequences that may not be as destructive as we now fear. In fact from a larger perspective, a child living the first two or three years of its life functionally separated from other peers may be more in violation of its biological-evolutionary past than the child reared in a communal peer environment.

Thus, though we know quite a bit about the parts adults, especially parents and teachers, play in learning and social role development, "the functions of peer relations are less clear. . . . In fact, most statements of functions in this regard must be considered merely assumptions now, with little if any systematic data available for support."[3]
Although the book began as a study of the influence of the peer group on learning, it was becoming evident by the end of the base year that the peer influence on academic performance in the classroom operated only among boys. Among girls in the primary grades the presence of a warm, supportive teacher seemed more closely related than peer influence to how well they did in school. The question, then, was why boys but not girls were so strongly influenced by peer-group effects. Answering this question seemed to require a closer study of the processes that differentiated the nature of social relationships among boys from those among girls. It was at this point that I began to see the relevance of the second—gender-role—curriculum to achievement in the first or academic curriculum.

The Second Curriculum: Gender-Role Socialization

For some time social psychologists and students of human development have been greatly preoccupied with the processes of socialization that prepare boys and girls for appropriate gender roles. Thus, along with the first, or academic, curriculum—reading, writing, and arithmetic—there was a second, or gender-role, curriculum in operation, which taught the children the traditional role behavior for their sex. It taught little girls to be helpful and nurturant. It taught little boys to distance themselves from girls, to look down on them, and to accept as their due the help that girls offered. Through its insistence that boys learn to be boys and girls learn to be girls, this

second curriculum resulted in separate worlds for the two sexes
within the classroom and on the playground. The boys' interpretation of the establishment norms of machismo forbade any recognition of or friendship with girls. It permitted no "sex relations," that
is, no relations between boys and girls.

The model that underlay my own thinking took this form: we
make inordinate demands on small boys to become instant men, to
live up to macho criteria they are as yet unprepared to meet (chapters 1–6). They have therefore to seek support from one another. The
same stresses are not imposed on girls. They do not have to become
instant women. They do not require as much strong peer-group support as do the boys.

The second curriculum did an effective job of teaching each sex
how to perform according to conventional gender norms and how to
live with members of its own sex. It was not as successful in teaching
the boys and girls how to relate to one another. How to live with the
other sex was far more difficult. This was a lesson the children
worked on by themselves with little help from adults. It was not part
of the school's design.

The Third Curriculum: Self-Taught "Sex Education"

As I worked my way through my observations on the boys and
girls, it became clear that there was another aspect of their development that—although I had recorded evidence of it—I had not
so far included in my analyses and interpretation. Scattered through
my notes were observations having to do with still another curriculum, this time a well-hidden one that the children were working
out for themselves. They knew it had to be kept sub rosa, because not
only did adults not supply it for them; they actually seemed to avoid
it. The children sensed and respected adult reticence in this matter
and protected adults from the third curriculum. They succeeded
well enough to have distracted me in my own detailed observations.
This curriculum had to do not with the way boys became boys or
girls, girls, but with the way they related to one another. It was a do-
it-yourself, self-taught education in sex relations. Unlike the first and
second adult-imposed curricula, this one was organized and
managed by the boys and girls themselves.

Although most adults had themselves gone through the third curriculum, they did not want to be reminded of its existence. When
they saw signs of it, they were punitive, either directly, in the form of
scolding, or indirectly, in the form of taunting. When they addressed
the issue at all they sent mixed messages.

Adults were explicit about the norms for physical and sexual relationships between the sexes. But regarding the more emotional and verbal aspects they were equivocal. Boys, for example, were taught by mothers and teachers that a gentleman was chivalrous and protective of girls. At the same time, from fathers and the media they learned that machismo called for taking sex when and where they could get it. Girls were taught one basic rule: Don't. Have as little to do with boys as possible. At the same time they were taught that it is important to win boys because being popular and dating are important. The children concluded that there were only two ways to relate to one another: hate or love, and love meant sex. Because of adult reluctance to tackle this curriculum head-on, there was little reported in the research literature on this finding. As I quarried my notes for clues, I wasn't so sure either school or parents would be eager to learn about it.

The first, or academic, curriculum, with the special problems it presented, especially to boys, was one I had wrestled with for many years. It was the second and third curricula that offered the new challenges. At the time I was observing the children there was considerable concern among parents and educators about sexism in schools. Textbooks, the media, and curricúla were all being scrutinized for evidence of a damaging sexist orientation that was limiting the sights of girls, restricting the emotional growth of boys, and establishing a nonegalitarian pattern of relationships between the sexes. This public concern suggested two possible innovations. One was to attempt, by challenging the stereotypes, to overcome the sexism that had characterized the children's schooling so far and revealed itself so blatantly in their acquisition of gender roles. The other would be an attempt to restructure the third curriculum to help the students learn how to relate to one another as friends rather than inevitably as potential sex partners. This would be far more difficult, for boy-girl friendships were not a part of the traditional socialization at Pine Hill. Though the atmosphere at that time did not encourage friendship between opposite-sex peers, I thought it should. Was it possible to open up such an alternative? Friendship rather than either "hate" or "love"? Was either innovation possible? This story supplies the answers.

PART ONE

The Importance of Peers

·1·

FORMATION OF GROUPS

Grade 1 Boys: Teacher Orientation

For both boys and girls, life in the kindergarten and first-grade classrooms at Pine Hill was tightly controlled by adults. This is how
the fourth-grader Michael, who as a first-grader had once called himself a "foxy football player," remembered his first day at school,
when his peers were as helpless as he was and only adults knew the
score:

> When I first walked into the school everyone looked so big to me.
> Later my teacher showed me around the classroom and I met my
> classmates. I sure was happy to find children that were my age and
> were the same size as me. Two boys walked over to me and said,
> "Hey, you! What's your name?" I just stood there and didn't even
> know what to say until I finally said, "Ah . . . ah . . . Wood . . . no,
> Wade. Michael Wade!" Then everyone stood silent and just stared at
> me with their bally eyes as if I were crazy.
>
> Then I met the principal and I couldn't see anything but his feet. I
> looked up to see his face and I tell you the truth I almost sprained my
> neck trying to look at his face. I was so nervous I shook from head to
> toe. When I had to tell him my name I thought I would faint.
>
> I could never remember my bus number so every day when school
> was out I couldn't find my school bus. I kept thinking that my bus
> number was 12,000 or 120,000,000 but it was only 12. When one of
> the patrols would ask me my bus number I just said, "Ah . . . ah . . .
> ah!" Then the kind old principal would ask me, "Do you know your
> bus number?" and I would tell him, "I . . . ah . . . I forgot it." Then the
> kind old principal got in touch with my bus number as quick as that!
> Boy, if it hadn't been for that kind old principal I would probably
> have missed my bus and never gotten home.

With peer relations as yet unformed, a child's only "ports in a storm"
were adults. It was to them, not to peers, that they looked for support. Like Michael, the other first-grade students were dependent on
the teacher not only for basic academic skills but for practical school

know-how: classroom routines, for example, had to be explained; they had to learn how to get their lunches and where they were to sit in the lunchroom; they needed to know how to find the bus that would take them home after school; they had to learn game rules and know which areas of the playground were designated for specific games. But there was also more, much more.

They needed not only simple coping help from the teacher but also her emotional support as they struggled to establish themselves as legitimate members of the school community. A gentle word from her was usually enough to persuade them to be cooperative and "good." In the first grade that I was observing, both boys and girls received such loving support from their teacher. They responded to her words of praise and hugs by wanting more. They sat on her lap and went to her rather than to peers for reassurance and support. Both of the first-grade teachers saw to it that the children maintained a good self-image even when being reminded that they had broken a class rule. The teacher was always in the picture.

Even the children's social life was characterized by a predominantly teacher-child rather than peer-child relationship. In the background of all the interactions among the children stood the watchful adult. Ms. Minor, for example, was in the habit of giving her children brief periods of play between work periods so that they could move about the room and chat with other children. They were engaged in one of these play periods one day near the end of December when Anne and Matthew began to shove each other away from the puzzle they were putting together. Ms. Minor noted that although the first few pushes and shoves had been friendly, they soon became hostile. "Anne and Matthew, come here to me," she called to them in a firm but affectionate voice. When they stood encircled in her arms she asked, "Can't you find another way to play?" The two children nodded their heads, indicating that they could. "Good! You're so good and I'm so happy with the way you've been playing, but you know that accidents can happen and someone might have to stay out of school. We wouldn't want that to happen, now would we?" Both children again shook their heads from side to side confirming that they certainly would not want that to happen. Ms. Minor then told the children that they could finish their puzzle. The children were pleased and happy. Their relationship with each other was far less important to them than their individual relationships with their teacher.

On another occasion, when two of the boys were in the beginning stages of a fight, Ms. Minor again called out for them to come to her. She put one arm around each of the boys and held them close to her. "Now let's watch the other children and see if anyone is hitting anyone else." They watched for a few seconds. "What do you see? Is anyone hitting anyone else?" No, they saw no one hitting others. "Look how well they're playing." They looked. "We have to watch because Ms. Minor has twenty-eight children and she can't watch all of them all of the time, can she?" The boys shook their heads; they agreed. "What can we do so that we can play safely together?" she asked. In unison they replied, "We can be good." "I knew you could," she crooned in a pleased and rewarding voice. Again the boys' relationship with each other was less important than their individual relationships with the teacher.

Still, the boys were beginning to recognize the importance of the peer group. The attitude was articulated by the first-grader Ryan in reply to a question from the teacher. "What would you do if your best friend didn't want to play with you?" "Well," he said thoughtfully, "if my best friend was playing with someone else I'd say, 'May I play, too?' I'd make friends with him, too." He then articulated the rule: "It's not good to have just one friend because what would you do if your friend went away or wasn't in school for three or four days? You wouldn't have anyone to play with." A fate, apparently, worse than death. The other boys agreed. Not to have anyone to play with? This was, indeed, "not good." Anything was better than that.

There was as yet no peer solidarity, no coalition of children against the establishment. The first-grade boys were still "co-optable." Before there could be any kind of structure among the children themselves there had to be at least partial emancipation from their teacher dependence. In the case of the boys I was observing it was to come in the second grade; in the case of the girls, not until the fourth.

Although the first-grade boys were beginning to learn what it meant to be a man according to the rules of the second curriculum, and although on occasion they defied a substitute teacher, they remained essentially teacher oriented throughout the first year. In second grade, however, there was a gradual shift—among the boys but not among the girls—in the direction of peer orientation. The boys became, in effect, weaned from the dependence that had marked the first year. They began, that is, to look to one another for support.

The Warrior Band

Among the second-grade boys whom I was observing, three important developmental processes relevant to group structure were taking place: (1) the individual transitions from teacher to peer orientation; (2) increasing sex segregation; and (3) a gradual establishment of a hierarchy. The effect of these processes was to produce, if not, as yet, a structured self-conscious group, a "pack" or "band," which came, in fact, to be known by adults as the Warrior Band.

Transition

Although at the beginning of the second grade there were occasional moments—particularly when no other children were around—when a second-grade boy might still permit the teacher to give him an affectionate hug, for most of the school day the boys maintained as much physical distance from the teacher as classroom space would allow. Boys who had complacently sat on their teacher's lap in the first grade now found such intimacy embarrassing.

The reorientation from teacher to peer did not happen instantly, and during the transitional period the old affectionate patterns between teacher and child came to be adapted to peer relationships. The boys freely showed affection for one another. Jim, for example, would walk up to another boy and hug him. Depending upon the circumstances and the mood of the hugged boy, he would either be hugged back or be told to go away. At Thanksgiving time, as the children were making turkeys out of pipe cleaners, paper cups, and brown bags, a cheerful holiday spirit prevailed. Several times Jim got up from his desk, walked a few steps to where another boy sat making his turkey, put his arms around him, and hugged him tightly. The other boys hugged back. But such expressions of warmth were becoming obsolete. Second-grade boys came in time to reject such overt displays of affection from peers as vehemently as they rejected them from the teacher.

As the potential for support from peers began to emerge, more and more of the boys began to find it possible to defy the teacher. When they behaved as independent agents and not as members of a group, they took the risk of severe punishment, as Scott learned the day the teacher asked him for his seat work and he said with considerable bravado, "I already gave it to you." Determined to call his bluff, the teacher asked, "When did you give it to me, Scott?" "When you were right over there," he said pointing to another part of the classroom. When the teacher replied that she did not remember receiving his seat work and doubted that he had given it to her he stood firm. "Well, I gave it to you. If you lost it don't blame me!" When the teacher subsequently found his paper crumpled into a ball inside his desk, Scott looked at the ceiling and then out the window as he hummed a little tune to himself. For this, Scott was sent out of the classroom and told to sit on the principal's bench. But now, unlike in the past, he was not alone. A procession of his peers on their way to the restroom risked punishment to visit with him on the bench. Such newly developing peer support was ample compensation for the time spent on the bench as well as for the scolding from the principal. Scott and his followers were beginning to learn the value of peer support.

The second-grade boys began the transition process from teacher to peer orientation early in the school year, so that by the spring of the year, they had completely transferred their need for rewards from their teacher to their peers. But the full significance of this process for learning did not strike me until I analyzed the routine test results for the second-grade children at the end of the year. The class as a whole had been progressing well until March, when the teacher became ill. In her absence, the children had a succession of substitute teachers who were unwilling or unable to cope with this class, which was reputed to be a "can of worms." Only one of the six substitute teachers remained longer than two weeks, and she stayed only six. It was not unexpected, then, that the children would suffer a learning setback during the term when they had had to adjust to so many teachers. There was regret but little surprise when the test results showed that nine of the twelve girls had lower test scores in June than in January, while the other three had merely held their own, with scores in the same range in June as in January. What was astonishing, however, and not only to me but to all those with whom I discussed it, was the finding that the academic achievement of the boys had not suffered any adverse effects whatsoever from the teacher's long-term absence. Eight of the twelve boys had scores in the same range in June as they had had in January. And four had even higher scores. None had suffered learning setbacks. All those who had lost ground in the teacher's absence were girls.

The boys' world had, apparently, protected them and provided them with stability during the disruptive succession of teachers. Among the girls, however, stability still depended upon the presence of a warm adult. Deprived of such support by the absence of the teacher, the girls did not seem to have, as the boys did, other resources. Their learning loss was thus greater.

Segregation

The second stage in the process of organizing the boys in the second grade was one of increasing segregation: that is, increased distancing from girls. This separatism was, they were learning, the most fundamental second-curriculum rule for male sex-role behavior. The school had no official system of sex segregation except in the conventional provision of separate toilet facilities. In the first grade the boys used their restroom as a refuge where they could momentarily escape from the stresses of the classroom. In the second grade it came to serve in addition as a congregating place, a kind of club room.

The assistant principal of a nearby elementary school once explained to me why boys spent so much time huddling in the restroom. It was, he said, a place where boys could escape the oppressive supervision of women teachers. And only the restroom guaranteed the boys the preferred companionship of their peers without the interference of girls in their activities.

Not all Pine Hill boys had the advantage of an exclusively male restroom. Boys in kindergarten and Head Start had to share the toilet facilities with the girls in their classrooms. A closed door ensured privacy, but there were many small boys who had to request help with zippers, belts, and suspenders, so that the presence of a female teacher in the restroom with a boy was not unusual. No kindergarten or Head Start boy at Pine Hill exhibited any kind of distress as the result of shared toilet facilities, possibly because everyone was used to sharing them with mothers and sisters at home.

The change in toilet procedures was almost immediate when the boys and girls at Pine Hill entered first grade. During the very first day of first grade, little girls were told to form one line, little boys another, and in these sex-segregated lines they were marched down the hall to the sex-segregated restrooms—possibly the single most significant symbols of the biological differences between boys and girls in the school.

It did not escape the attention of the children that while the teacher walked freely in and out of the girls' restroom to stop loud talking or to bring out a girl who stayed inside to play, she never went into the boys' restroom. Instead she would stand outside the door and call out to the boys to "stop fighting" or to "come out here immediately" if they stayed too long inside. When this approach failed to produce a boy, the principal would be summoned to "go in and get him." A first grade boy's defiance of his teacher's commands—if only for a few seconds' duration—put him in charge of his own actions and gained for him the admiration of peers. It was a heady moment. But when he came face-to-face with the teacher an explanation was in order. "I wasn't finished" or "I was still on the toilet" were among the most common excuses offered.

A child's right to visit the toilet was not limited to routinized times decided upon by the teacher. First-grade boys regularly used the restroom as a momentary escape from the classroom and they

visited it several times a day, though seldom staying for a long period of time. Some first-grade boys used it as a place to play with
boys they met there on a chance basis or to watch the gatherings of
older boys; frequently they had to be led protesting back to the classroom.

In the second grade, however, the congregating of two or three or
more boys in the restroom ceased to be a chance event. It became,
rather, a planned one. One boy would leave the room with the
teacher's permission and other boys would sneak out the door to join
him. Later, boys did not attempt to sneak out of the room but made
plans to rendezvous openly by spacing their requests and trusting
that the teacher would not notice that the other boys had not yet
returned. If the teacher did notice what was happening and did not
grant a request to leave the room, the boy would pretend to be in the
worst possible agony and, clutching his crotch, would tell her, "I
have to go real bad." This ploy worked every time, for no Pine Hill
teacher—as the boys well knew—would risk having a boy wet his
pants. But there were times when a teacher, knowing that the boy
had just returned from the lavatory, questioned the validity of his
request. On one of these occasions a third-grade boy, eager to get
back to the restroom so that he would not miss out on any of the fun,
replied angrily, "I've been potty trained since I was a baby and I
know when I have to go and when I don't and I have to go real bad."

The meetings in the restroom became, increasingly, an important
part of the boys' school day, for there—protected from intrusion by
girls or women—they plotted and planned their all-male activities.
When I asked the boys what they did in the restroom that took so
much time, they told me that they talked about other kids in the
school and about what they would do for the rest of the day, decid-
ing such important matters as "whose ball we're going to hijack at
Free Play," and "if we should run up and down the halls and slide
on the bannister." From the school principal I learned, also, that the
boys used the restroom to see who could urinate highest up the wall.
To the boys at Pine Hill, the restroom was the single most important
room in the school.

Another locale of segregation was the lunchroom. Here as in the
lavatory the boys were free of the teacher, although under the supervision of teacher aides. But here segregation by sex was not, as in the
case of the lavatory, imposed by the school. Classes of children were
assigned to specific tables in the lunchroom, and table hopping between classes was forbidden. Because of their small class size the
two first-grade classes shared three long tables, while two tables per
classroom were allocated to children in grades two through six. Following teacher instructions the first-grade boys sat side-by-side with

girls, but as the second-grade boys began to segregate themselves from girls in the classroom and on the playground, they also began to claim one end of the tables for themselves, leaving the other end for the girls. By third grade the boys would run to the cafeteria to claim one lunch table for "boys only," and girls, having no choice, sat at the other. It was here that the boys made their final plans for the outdoor play that followed lunch time, and those plans did not include girls.

A third segregated region was, like the lavatory, institutionalized by the school. A large part of the play area was allocated to the space requirements of the boys' games. Segregation was thus imposed on the children, for it was made quite clear that specific blacktop and grassy areas were designed for ball games—viewed by teachers and children alike as boys' games—while the fringe areas were deemed sufficient for hopscotch and jump-rope games assigned to girls. But the segregation was not nearly as rigid as with the lavatories. Girls did try to invade male turf. At times there was, in fact, a "battle of the sexes," as boys chased away girls who wanted to play ball games. Some girls earned the right to play, but less persistent girls were intimidated by the boys, who told them that they were unfit for the ball field. Segregation in the lunchroom and on the playground thus conferred "top dog" status on boys while assigning girls to the lesser status of second-class citizens.

A different kind of segregation—this time on the basis not of sex but of age—also took place on the playground and served as another principle of organization among second-grade boys. They were no longer "low men on the totem pole" but seasoned students with status in the school and with corresponding privileges and territorial rights. As now advanced, established school members they began to use their fists and feet to establish and defend their own turf. The cautious approach they had shown in the first grade outside the classroom was now replaced by a bolder spirit. They began to explore beyond the range of their teacher's influence and to play in areas where the second- and third-grade children had played the previous year. They thus strengthened the bonds among themselves for protection against other forces in the school.

Hierarchy

Along with distancing from teachers and segregation from girls there was a third step in the organizational process, the emergence of hierarchical patterns among the boys. Maccoby and Jacklin raise an interesting point on this aspect of the process: "The fact that boys travel in larger groups [than girls] probably has considerable significance. We suspect that the size of social groups has a great deal to do with dominance patterns. Large social groups cannot so easily function without a dominance hierarchy as can small groups."[1] The importance of being first, of establishing leadership in the group that arose among the second-grade boys, will be discussed in more detail in chapter 6. We note here that the criteria for first place varied. Sean, for example, proved his right to be the first captain of the ball team in the time-honored way of "beating up" any boy who challenged him. Ranking on the basis of superior academic performance also took place and undoubtedly contributed to the boys' success in learning during the series of substitute teachers in the spring of the school year.

Reorientation from teacher to peers in social relationships, segregation in the restroom, lunchroom, and playground, and the emphasis on hierarchical order were all related to the developmental processes that were to eventuate in the emergence of a structured group, the Tent Club, in the third grade. But not all boys were equally involved. There were some who never made it "in."

·2·

THE TENT CLUB

To the first- and second-grade boys had fallen the task of establishing the criteria that determined a boy's mastery of the second curriculum. As they grew older they demanded of one another increasingly higher performance standards. If running the forty-yard dash was an acceptable standard for a first-grade boy, then a third-grade boy could be expected to run the sixty-yard dash in record time. A six-year-old boy could earn peer approval merely by standing up to his teacher, but a third-grade boy had to demonstrate greater inventiveness in his defiance of the establishment. First-grade boys shared their lunchroom table with the girls in their class with no loss of macho points, but the third-grade boys had to defy school rules as they raced to the cafeteria to lay claim to a table where only boys would be permitted to sit. Although everyone did his best to impress his peers, not all primary boys passed the tests with flying colors.

A boy who met the criteria for machismo established by the peer group was rewarded with acceptance. He was viewed by them as a man among men, thus reinforcing the self-image he had worked so hard to achieve. He would be permitted to try his skill on the ball field against that of his peers so that he could maintain his status as a real man. He would be permitted physical contact with other boys who passed the tests, such as walking on the playground with his arm around another boy's shoulders. He would be included in the antiestablishment activities of the groups, thus further affirming his machismo. Being accepted as a man meant also that he would never have to resort to the companionship of girls.

There were, however, in every grade level boys who seemed to fail no matter how hard they tried. Since the precise criteria used to determine a boy's success or failure in the second curriculum had not been spelled out, the boys had to pick up on cues that would tell them what it was they must do to be regarded as real men. For the majority of the boys this seemed a relatively simple task, but for others it seemed impossible. A misinterpretation of the cues led some boys to engage in inappropriate behavior that resulted in punishment by peers who would not play with them.

Cast suddenly into a world whose cues they either did not catch or did not know how to respond to, they found themselves "outsiders." At Pine Hill the first- and second-grade boys who experienced this painful situation may never have learned what was wrong; at least they never lost hope that they would eventually be accepted by peers. But in the third grade, with standards for machismo firmly established, the boys themselves would become able to articulate who was "in" and who was "out." In the first and second grades it had been "every man for himself," but in the third grade the "in" boys were to band together, in a newly organized Tent Club, and were thus to be in a position to demand that peers either conform to their model for machismo or be rejected, cast out from the larger group. Now there would be no second chances for the "outsiders." This one decision—to admit a boy to membership in the Tent Club or to deny him access to the activities of the peer group—was to have profound effects on the social life and the academic performance of every boy in the third grade at Pine Hill. The line would be clearly drawn between the winners and losers.

Up to this point in their development the boys had been responding to the demands of the second—or gender-role—curriculum as dictated by parents, teachers, the media, and books. They had needed the support of a strong peer group while they were working out their own version of it, and they would continue to need that support. But by the time they reached the third grade they were well enough indoctrinated in the lessons of the second curriculum to become their own enforcers of its prescriptions and proscriptions. The Tent Club, which had been in the process of development for the past two years, was to be their vehicle.

With the exception of the boys who were new to the third-grade classroom in September 1973, I had known all of the eight-year-old boys when they were second-graders. When they had left for summer vacation in the spring of 1973 they had seemed very young, still small children. When they returned to school in the fall, only two and a half months later, they had changed; they seemed to have put the insecurities of early childhood behind them, to emerge as "modern men." With their newfound confidence they learned how to organize and how to use the power they had gained by being an organized group against the establishment.

There was, however, continuity as well as change. The "I'm first!" game was, for example, a holdover from the previous year. In the first month of school the boys continued to play it everywhere and under all kinds of circumstances. Even when the school bell rang and they would have preferred to remain outside, they headed for the school door at top speed, pushing one another out of the way and shouting as they neared the door, "I'm first!" "I'm second!" "I'm third!" and so on until they were all inside the classroom.

But in October, when the rest of the class had caught up with them, their triumphant cries changed abruptly. It began to dawn on them that this competitive game might sometimes play into the hands of authority. Why should they rush pell-mell to go inside? "We had a great game going outside and our side was winning. If we had stayed out a little longer we could have won that game!" If they had worked together as a team instead of competing as individuals to be first in getting inside, they could have finished the game. Like adult competitors in many walks of life, they were beginning to understand the power of organization.

They came to use their power in the classroom also. When I first discussed with the teachers in the primary grades my hunch that there was some kind of relationship between membership or exclusion from the boys' peer group and the learning process—particularly as it affected reading achievement—they were eager to help the boys in their classrooms achieve peer acceptance. It seemed to them a simple answer: they would insist that every boy in their classroom be included in the activities of the peer group. I did not agree. I had not yet confirmed my hunch to my own satisfaction. I had no way of knowing as yet who would be excluded or for how long or what the results of exclusion would be. Even if my hunch were confirmed we did not know the cause or what to do about it. Nevertheless, one of the third-grade teachers, despite my urgent request that she not interfere with the classroom process, went ahead anyway. She did not permit the group to follow its own structure. She changed the classroom seating arrangement to assure maximum contact among all the boys in the class. The consequences were disastrous. The classroom responded as though it had been dealt a mortal blow. It reeled. The next morning the protests from the boys were loud and insistent. Amid confusion, shouting, arguing, and fighting the boys pushed their desks around the room until the seating arrangement again reflected the group structure as they experienced it.

"I want to sit beside Chad," Derek shouted at the teacher as he pushed his desk across the room. Chad wanted to sit beside Billy, who at that time was the high-status boy in the class—an honor he owed to his ability to "beat up" any boy who challenged him. Tommy ran around the room chased by Ronnie. Dismayed, the teacher tried to distract the boys by pointing to a beautiful aquarium she had purchased and assembled the previous evening as a surprise for the class. "Look at the beautiful fish in your aquarium," she urged. "What color are the fish?" The boys stopped and looked at the fish. They answered her question. But the respite gained by this ploy was only momentary, for the confusion resumed as Billy took his books out of the desk assigned him and moved them to the desk beside Jeffrey. Jonathan put his books in the desk beside Paul. Ronnie and Derek began to fight. "I'd rather be any place in the world than beside that pig!" Ronnie shouted to demonstrate his contempt for this new boy who had not yet been accepted by peers. It was not long before all the boys in the room had moved their desks or their books to another place in the room. Only then were they willing to show the good manners the teacher was calling for. They sat down. But they had shown me and the teacher—and also themselves—that the group already had a latent structure.

At the beginning of the school year the structure of the classroom group I was observing in the third grade was unclear. Membership was undefined. All the boys in the class hoped and fought for the right to belong to a group with unfixed boundaries. Everyone could still hope. Thus, on an interest inventory administered to the class in November—dealing, among other topics, with friends—Tommy, Jeffrey, Nicky, Chad, Billy, Jonathan, and Paul had chosen one another as "best friends." Paul's list had also included the name of a boy new to the class, Derek. But not one of these boys had named Ronnie, Denver, Kenny, or Jason on their "best friends" list. Still not recognizing, or unwilling to recognize, their exclusion, the unselected boys specified as among their "best friends" such popular boys as Paul, Nicky, and Jonathan; Jeffrey, Billy, and Chad.

It was not until the middle of the year—in early December—that the structure of the group jelled and the boys themselves became aware of it. It might well be said that the organization of the Tent Club marked the discovery of the group rather than its formation. Not until then had the boys articulated who was in and who was out. But now, with a name, the group became "official." The Tent Club was more than a network of "best friends." It was to be a secret club whose membership would be limited to the original members— Chad, Paul, Jonathan, and their friends. Before the month was over Billy, Jeffrey, Nicky, and Tommy had also become members. As had Derek. He had asked if he could belong and Jonathan had told him that he could. But Ronnie, who also wanted to join and asked if he could, was not accepted. No, they already had "too many guys." So Ronnie, Denver, Kenny, and Jason lost out; they were not allowed in. The choices made by the boys for the interest inventory had been remarkably predictive of what was actually happening now. It became increasingly clear that Denver, Ronnie, Jason, and Kenny were not to be included in the activities of the peer group. The latent structure now became manifest.

The organization of the Tent Club was the culmination of a long process of proving manhood in an all-male arena. Beginning in prototypical form in the first grade, this process had transformed a bunch of disparate little individuals, still strongly adult-oriented in the first grade, into a "band" or "pack" in second grade and, now, in the third, into a well-structured group. Once the group was a reality, the boys began to see themselves less in terms of one-to-one relationships and more as parts of a larger, self-conscious group. The individual competitiveness that had begun to fix rank before the group became aware of itself became modified. United they could flout some of the establishment demands. They could impose their own social order on the boys in the classroom despite their teacher's attempts to change it. They could reconstruct the power structure, changing the criteria for top position. The effects on the boys, both members and those excluded from membership, were to be profound.

Machismo was a compelling force throughout the year. The boys in grades one and two had absorbed their macho code from the media (especially television), textbooks, and library books, from their Boy Scout code, and from adult models at home and at school. The third-grade boys insisted on compliance with this macho model to a far greater extent than did the younger boys. For a third-grade boy to be labeled a sissy, for example, was a fate worse than death. He would go to any length to avoid it. Being a cry-baby was intolerable in a boy. Being too oriented toward female adults, whether mothers or teachers, was also inexcusable. Aggressive violence, an acceptable and even necessary display of machismo in second grade, was not called for by the macho model in the third, but defending oneself against aggression was. Even Billy, who had depended upon his fighting ability to control the group in second grade, began to get the messsage that fighting per se was not in.

Perhaps because of its middle-class character or perhaps because reading as an activity now enjoys greater status (President Kennedy once took a speed-reading course) reading at Pine Hill was not viewed as a sissy occupation, as it reportedly is in some schools. Tommy, for example, could be a bookworm and get away with it. True, reading was not a macho thing to do in the same sense as playing ball, but it was important, as were good grades. The boys who were rejected from peer-group membership lost macho points because they were reading "baby" books—first- and second-grade readers—while other boys read at or above grade-level expectancy for their age group.

On the positive side, machismo meant being competitive, assertive, determined to win. It meant being first. It meant being a good
ball player; in playing anything it meant playing rough. It meant
being able to take it. It meant defying the establishment, especially
the female half of it. This was the macho canon.

Once the Tent Club had discovered itself, it used a variety of
techniques to cement its identity, to delimit clearly who was in and
who was not. Two of the most important practices were the telling of
secrets shared only by members and the use of "in" names.

Secrets

In his discussion of men in groups Lionel Tiger concludes that
secrets play a not inconsiderable part in male bonding. The boys in
the third grade, without benefit of erudite research, confirmed this
conclusion. The Tent Club had a secret the day after it was organized. Since I was a charter member of the club, I was permitted to
ask what the secret was. "We have only one so far," Chad told me,
and when he did not elaborate I prodded further. "I don't remember
what it is," said Chad, looking uncomfortable. But Jonathan poked
Chad in the side and prompted, "You remember, RJJ and G." "Oh,
yeah," Chad agreed as he shifted his weight from one foot to the
other but still did not tell me the secret. "But what does it mean?" I
asked. There was reluctance to reply but finally Jonathan decoded
the message: "Retarded Jason Jenkins and all the girls." "Do you
think Jason is retarded?" I asked. "Yeah, and all the girls, too," they
said. Apparently embarrassed, Chad tugged on Jonathan's arm and
urged him, "Come on, we have to get outside." The *idea* of secrets as
a way of expressing "in-ness" was more important than what they
were about.

The inclusion of "all the girls" with the allegedly "retarded" boy
was in line with the segregating process that had begun in the first
grade. The Tent Club was in league with all the forces that might
challenge the boys' maleness. Secrets helped to draw the line.

In-Names

Another technique for strengthening in-group identity and clearly
marking boundaries between members and nonmembers was an in-
group game consisting of adding a long e to a boy's name. Thus, for
example, Chad became Chaddy. When I asked the boys why, they
had no ready answer except, "Everyone calls him Chaddy." And,
Chad added, "We call Derek 'Derry.'" "What do you call Paul?"
"Pauly," they replied. "And Tommy is Tommy." When I asked what
they called Denver, a name not easy to add a long e onto, they

replied, "Oh, him. We don't care about him. He's not in our gang."
"Who else is not in your gang?" I asked. "Kenny and Ronnie." They
were apparently so far out that even names ending with an *e* sound
were irrelevant. (Jason had moved to another school district by this
time—late February—and Edward had not yet enrolled in Pine Hill.)
This was the first time the "in" boys had articulated who was in and
who was not. The use of an in-name made it official that Ronnie,
Denver, and Kenny did not belong. Neither, of course, did any of the
girls.

Although the in-boys knew which boys were out, they could not
state precisely what standards they had used in excluding them.
However, the names the in-boys called the excluded boys—sissy,
cry-baby, mama's boy, for example—revealed the criteria implicit in
their judgments. The excluded boys, not given in-names, were regarded as being like girls and not like real men.

The Tent Club boys bonded not only against girls and boys they
considered "sissies" but also against the establishment. The Tent
Club was, in fact, an aggressive antiestablishment weapon. It helped
members circumvent the rules of the school. It might, for example,
have been difficult to tell Ronnie, Kenny, and Jason that they could
not play ball with them. The excluded boys could legitimately complain to the teacher, who would then ask embarrassing questions,
such as why these boys were excluded, or make unwelcome demands that they be included. But it was easy to tell the excluded
boys themselves that they could not belong to their secret club. Who
could object to that?

The Tent Club also facilitated antiestablishment activities. In the
second grade the antiestablishment fun had been fairly harmless.
Once during an art lesson, for example, second-grade boys had
kicked sponges around the room because "it looked like fun so we
did it." When they should have been concentrating on their reading
lessons, they sometimes poked one another in the ribs and joked
about private matters in an interpersonal but unorganized way. Or
they might run into the library and hide from their teacher because
they considered it fun.

In the third grade, however, defying authority became a major
form of fun; but it was harder. The boys had to work for this kind of
fun. And it required group effort. During a snowstorm, for example,
they rolled enormous snowballs across the entrance to the school
parking lot, where they froze during the night so that no cars could
get into the lot the following morning. Watching the confusion that
followed as teachers tried to find parking on the snowbound streets
was fun for the boys. On another occasion Derek led the peer group

boys in throwing mud balls at the houses and cars in their neighborhood, and that was fun even though they had to clean up the mess they had caused. They inserted pieces of metal and wood into the school's light switches, running the risk of electrocution. After turning out the lights they would stay in the dark lavatory and attempt to frighten the younger boys as they came unsuspectingly through the door. They had food battles in the cafeteria and they threw snowballs at other children, although they knew they were sure to be punished for such deeds.

One of the most creative and enterprising antiestablishment acts was carried out under the direction of Jonathan. The boys brought buckets of sand to school late one spring afternoon and poured them into the casings of open windows on the downstairs level of the school. Attempts to close the windows kept teachers and custodians in the school until five and six o'clock in the evening. That idea brought Jonathan such acclaim from peers that he went one step further. Shortly after the end of the children's school day, Jonathan and the Tent Club boys returned and stuffed paper in the school locks so that they would shut but would not open the following morning. They looked forward to the cancellation of school the next day. That was fun until they discovered that a hastily called locksmith was able to remove the locks so that school could start on time. These kinds of fun were imaginative and required the courage to defy authority, but carrying them out also called for group support.

The Tent Club served still another function. It distributed power more evenly among the boys within the group. It would, for example, reduce Billy's preeminence soon after its organization. Early in the year Billy had made it clear that since he was the best ball player in the class and the best fighter to boot, he would be in charge of making the decisions in ball games. He and only he would be in charge of the ball. Dealing with the boys one by one, he could easily enforce his claims. But when the boys became organized, no longer dealing with Billy as isolated individuals, he could no longer dominate them. Chad was a case in point.

Early in the third grade Chad had attached himself with seemingly total devotion to Billy. When Billy had commanded, Chad had obeyed. He had fought for Billy, cleaned up for him, supported his decisions. In return, Billy gave Chad something he valued highly: a close relationship with and the protection of the toughest and, at that time, most popular boy in the class. Chad became sought after by other boys because he was a lifeline to Billy. He was a "friend in court."

This relationship with Billy continued after the organization of the Tent Club. Then, as he became secure in his relationship with other Tent Club boys—Paul, Jonathan, Jeffrey, Nicky, Derek, and Tommy—Chad no longer needed Billy's patronage. He had made it. He could now insist, tauntingly, that he had only "fake-liked" Billy; that Billy had been deceived into believing that he had really been a devoted follower and admirer. Chad explained how "fake-liking" worked. "Sometimes you have to 'fake-like' a guy so that when the guys you really like aren't around you have him to play with." When driven to desperate measures a boy would "fake-like" even an excluded boy rather than chance having to resort to girls for companionship. If Chad was the beneficiary of "fake-liking," Billy was the victim of it. The fact that Chad had only "fake-liked" Billy before the Tent Club was organized and that Billy had fallen for it was held against him, while Chad's cleverness in exploiting him was admired. To have been taken in by Chad was, implicitly, a negation of Billy's machismo.

Chad was only the first to defect from Billy's leadership. Once the boys became secure in their group identity, they in effect dethroned Billy. In-group struggles for leadership rights and decision-making rights continued, but the power now came to be distributed among members of the group in a familiar manner; that is, they had a first captain, a second captain, a third captain, etc., until everyone was ranked. But rank now depended upon the activity of the group and the skill of a particular boy in carrying out that activity.

The consequences for Billy of his fall from power were noticeable. The playground aide, a young college student, remarked that Billy was showing "withdrawal symptoms" from the loss of the exclusive adulation of his peers. "I have a lot of trouble with Billy on the playground now. Other kids are always coming to tell me that Billy hit them or took their ball away or something like that. Or Billy will come and tell me that someone is bothering him. In the fall when the kids played Greek dodge ball Billy would organize the game but they don't play Greek dodge ball so much now so he doesn't have so much to do." I asked if she thought any other boy in the group had become a stronger leader than Billy. She thought not. "No, I couldn't pick out any one boy. They all seem to play together."

Thus, in one way or another, the in-boys established their own world with its own macho dynamic. The boys who as little first-graders, still not quite emancipated from the female world, had organized into fluid relationships, who as second-graders had become a band, well on the way to complete segregation from the female world, had now, in the third grade, become members of an organized, self-conscious, structured male group. They were now novitiates, "men in groups," participants in male bonding.

Penalties of Exclusion

For the boys who did not make it into the Tent Club, however, the story was different. They were, literally, losers. As the months passed and the Tent Club became more solidly entrenched, the gulf between the two groups widened. The decision to exclude Ronnie, Denver, Kenny, Jason, and later Edward was final. There were to be no second chances for them. The penalties of exclusion grew more destructive both to themselves and to others.

Exclusion by the Tent Club deprived the boys of full participation in the play and social activities of the peer group. The one arena in which they could establish themselves as men was now permanently closed to them. They might, on occasion, be permitted to play ball with the in-boys because another "man" was needed for the game, but they were not to reap the rewards of winning—the assurance by peers that they were real men.

Exclusion deprived them of something even more important: friends. It meant that the only choices of companionship now available to the excluded boys were among themselves. They became a group not by choice but by default. Despite common experiences they did not willingly associate with one another. They did not even like one another—who likes a loser?—and they were often explicit in their expressions of dislike. Thus Ronnie, speaking of the other rejected boys, said, "They think I like them but I don't." And on one occasion when Ronnie, Denver, and Jason were waiting in the school hall for Kenny, who had stayed behind in the library, Kenny said to me, "Do you hear them out there? They're waiting for me. They think I'm their best friend but I'm not. I don't even like them."

Their contacts were often characterized by taunts and conflicts. Kenny, who did not like to fight at all, once taunted Denver with, "Remember when I beat you up?" Denver, who was bigger and stronger than Kenny, asked incredulously, "When did you beat me up?" "Don't you remember?" Kenny then turned to Ronnie to provide a safety valve against being beaten up by Denver. "Denver told me yesterday that he can't stand you," Kenny said. "Wh-at?" cried Denver, becoming angry with Kenny. "Yes, you did, Denver," Kenny persisted. "Remember when Ronnie wasn't listening?"

Even their teacher was puzzled by these uncongenial groupings. It seemed strange to her that the boys spent so much time together, "because," she said, "they really don't like one another. They are always glad when one of them is absent. They say, 'I'm glad he's not here today. Now maybe I can get my work done.'" The explanation was not complex. They huddled together because they needed support and companionship from someone, and there was no one else to supply it.

There was one last resort: girls. And it was the ultimate penalty of exclusion that the boys had to resort to girls for companionship. Less exclusionary than boys, the girls accepted them without question. The resulting mixed-sex grouping was not a congenial group like the Tent Club nor yet a warm relationship like a friendship. It was, rather, what could be called a "companionate." If a stigma as serious as "sissy" had not been placed on boys who played with girls, they would have been able to admit to themselves and others that they liked the company of girls.

This positive attitude toward girls contrasted sharply with the rejection of girls that characterized the "male bond" among the in-group boys. Whereas the in-boys' idea of fun was "the rougher the game, the greater the fun," the rejected boys' ideas of fun had to include the milder form of playing with girls. The in-boys perceived girls as not good enough to play with. Girls should make up their own games and leave boys' games alone, they thought. The rejected boys, already excluded from the boys' world, where one competed for the rewards of maleness, had less to lose when they played with girls. Humiliating as it might be to have to stoop so low, it was better than nothing at all.

They could, however, salvage one component of the macho world for themselves. They could boast—however defensively—about the fun they had kissing the girls. In this arena they could again feel macho pride. The relationship with girls could project more than a companionate; it permitted some macho points. The pursuit of sexual contact with girls was permitted by the macho code; they could thus show that they regarded girls as sex objects and not as friends.

So much then, for the rewards some boys attained and the penalties some suffered from the way their world operated.

Family and Class as Factors in Group Status

It was not possible for me to unravel all the threads in this complex fabric of relationships. Much of a boy's position in the group might be attributable to personality characteristics. But the objection may be legitimately raised that in the attempt here to communicate on the world of the children themselves, family and class factors at work in the processes determining group status have been blotted out, and parents hover only vaguely in the background, intruding in the children's worlds only occasionally. Since research has shown the primary significance of the family on child development, some attention to family background and class status is called for here. It might shed some light on the findings about group membership.

Family as a Factor

All the boys in the third grade lived in two-parent families and all were living with their biological parents. In only four cases, those of Derek, Chad, Ronnie, and Jason, did the mother as well as the father work outside the home. Jeffrey and Kenny's mothers supplemented the family income by providing child-care services in their home for both preschool and school-age children. The parents of the boys, both mothers and fathers, demonstrated an active interest in their academic progress and were supportive of teachers and other school staff members.

Ronnie's parents were deeply concerned that he have access to a good school: they had moved into the area served by Pine Hill because they had heard that the school had "loving" teachers. They became involved with the PTA, helped Ronnie with his homework when he needed assistance, and never missed a scheduled conference with the teacher. Jason was involved with his family to an extraordinary extent. Perhaps one of the factors in his rejection by peers was that Jason frequently wept openly in the classroom and, when questioned, said that he missed his mother or was worried about her well-being. Edward clung, physically and emotionally, to his mother even at school where he could be observed by peers. Because she worked in the school as a volunteer, spending much of her time in Edward's own classroom, Edward was able to run to her to complain when other boys tested him for machismo. His clinging, his complaints to his mother about his peers, and her interference in their affairs undoubtedly cost him group membership. His peers labeled him a "mama's boy."

Denver's mother was active in the PTA and his father was a substitute coach for a Little League team to which several of the peer-group boys belonged. Denver was the youngest of four children and the only boy in his family. His sisters had been good students, and his mother, contrasting Denver's performance in school with theirs, occasionally remarked that "Denver must have cotton stuffed between his ears." She was clearly prouder of her daughters than of her son, who disgraced her by failing to learn to read. Tommy's father was also a Little League coach and president of the PTA. His sister was captain of the school patrols, a brilliant student, and an outstanding ball player. *Jonathan's* father, kept away from home for weeks at a time by a demanding job, had little communication with Jonathan. His mother, although deeply concerned with all aspects of Jonathan's life, consciously maintained almost total physical distance from her son when she worked in the school as a volunteer. *Billy's* mother encouraged his use of fighting to maintain dominance in his peer group. She found his reduction in rank to "one of the boys" after the formation of the Tent Club unbearable. In fourth grade her hostility toward Jonathan probably did more than any other factor to create a situation in which Billy could no longer function successfully within the peer group. With his peer relations in disarray, Billy was "promoted" to fifth grade toward the end of the school year to ease the constant friction within the classroom and on the playground. That act cost him his membership in the Tent Club. The fifth grade in-boys, while they might have noted his fourth-grade machismo, never accepted him as a bona fide fifth-grader, nor did they admit him to their company. Billy struggled with his new situation without complaint and when he saw his former peers in the Tent Club he bragged about the accomplishments that had led to his "promotion."

Jeffrey's father was a stern man whose ambitions for his son went no further than a high-school diploma. His mother was a quiet, shy woman who was uncomfortable among teachers. Jeffrey was the younger of two boys, and his brilliant older brother would anticipate what it was that Jeffrey would learn next in school and teach it to him at home. Thus Jeffrey was always ahead of his classmates. Jeffrey knew the importance of good grades, for it was his ambition to win a scholarship to a military academy and thereby escape a life of relative poverty. *Paul's* father tended to be critical of the school when teachers or the principal had to spend time counseling the students rather than teaching them. Counseling was his job; educating them was the teacher's job. Paul's mother was actively engaged in a number of social activities, but she found time to devote to the school. *Nicky's* mother was the class's "room mother," and she helped with field trips and classroom parties. His father was supportive of the school but did not participate in its activities.

Derek's father had adult children from a previous marriage who lived in another state. He was a strict disciplinarian. In his father's presence Derek was a model of good behavior, while among his peers he was an "idea man" whose antics led the Tent Club boys into frequent confrontations with neighbors and the school. Derek and his sisters were "latchkey kids" and, as such, had to be accountable for their own behavior for several hours after school each day. Their home, directly across the street from Pine Hill, made it possible for them to spend much of that time either in the school or on the playground. Kenny's family was large and poor, but they would not accept free tuition for Kenny's summer school classes and they arranged for his transportation to and from the school each day. Both of Chad's parents worked outside the home, but his mother found time to help with school activities. He was the third of five boys in the family, and his two older brothers, both strong athletes, must have provided excellent models for the macho role he played so well.

All of the boys' parents regarded the ability to read well as essential to a successful school career and all were willing to provide personal help as well as any other necessary resources, such as summer school. Family background per se did not appear to be the cause of group exclusion. However, excessively close ties to mothers did seem related, at least in the cases of Edward and Jason, to loss of macho points and thus loss of membership in the peer group. As Hartup pointed out, ". . . dependency on adults may interfere with popularity." Particularly dependency on mothers.

Class as a Factor

Although in the base year of the study Pine Hill was fairly homogeneous as far as racial composition was concerned, both blue-collar and white-collar backgrounds were represented among the students. The Tent Club included boys from both backgrounds, but every one of the excluded boys was blue-collar with the exception of the sole white-collar boy not accepted in the Tent Club.

The impact of class can be studied in terms of the neighborhoods in which the boys lived. Figure 1 offers suggestive clues in this connection. It will be noted that three of the excluded boys lived in neighborhood 3, known as "Olde Towne" to residents of the area. Two of them—Kenny and Jason—lived close together, but isolated from the other boys in their class. Of the cluster of boys—Chad, Jeffrey, Nicky, and Denver—who lived on the same street in this blue-collar area, all except Denver were Tent Club members. After-school contacts with peers were severely limited for Ronnie, another excluded boy, who lived in an apartment complex in neighborhood 2. Edward, the only boy from a white-collar family to be excluded, lived in the neighborhood of Pine Hill, in close proximity to five of the Tent Club boys.

Among primary-age boys it is not easy to ascertain the way class might have operated as a factor in the selection of boys for the Tent Club, and the boys themselves were of little direct help. If class per

FIGURE 1

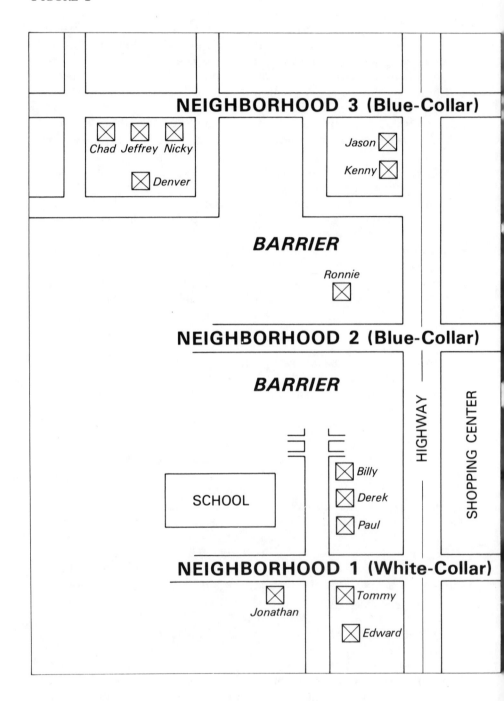

se were the important factor, then Jeffrey, Chad, Nicky, and Denver should not have been members of the peer group, but of these four boys only Denver was excluded. (Low) social class was neither a necessary nor a sufficient condition for determining membership or nonmembership in the Tent Club.

Feinberg and his associates report class differences among adolescents that are difficult to interpret. When adolescents from low- and middle-income families were asked what criteria they used for accepting others as peers, they emphasized common interests, the ability to talk well, and the tendency to mind one's own business. A propensity for fighting, on the other hand, was cause for rejection. Adolescents from high-income groups emphasized competitiveness, leadership, participation in activities, cheerfulness, and scholarship as criteria for acceptance, and low IQ, lack of leadership, failure to participate in activities, and immaturity as reasons for rejection.[1]

When the primary-age boys at Pine Hill were older and more mature, they, too, valued those characteristics deemed necessary for social acceptance by Feinberg's high-income adolescent group. But for first-, second-, and third-graders, fighting—in particular, the willingness to fight when challenged—was an important, even necessary, proof of machismo. Common interests and the ability to mind one's own business were also important for gaining membership in the peer group. At this time in their lives the children considered age differences more important than class differences; they lacked the social skills of Feinberg's adolescent groups regardless of their socioeconomic backgrounds. Perhaps at the ages of six, seven, and eight, children are less aware of class differences than they are when they get older. At Pine Hill, at any rate, this appeared to be the case.

·3·

WINNERS AND LOSERS

An outside observer might not have been able to understand why some boys were winners and others losers. Ronnie was a strong, well-built nine-year-old child who played ball as well as any of the boys, but he was rejected by his peers, while Tommy, whose slight build and scholarly bent of mind should have made him a loser, had no trouble gaining peer acceptance. The brief sketches of the third-grade boys in Table 1 show them as their peers saw them: as "men among men" or as "outsiders."

Jonathan

Jonathan was a *role transcender*. That is, he had both macho and nurturant characteristics. On the macho side he could play ball with the best, he could run fast, he was an imaginative leader in games, he was competitive both on the playground and in the classroom, and he could defy the establishment and perform all the other acts appreciated in the macho world of boys. But on the nurturant side, he could also be understanding, helpful, and even loving and openly affectionate with friends. The gentler side was not held against him as it might have been were he a boy with less obvious macho power. By the end of the school year he had emerged as the best-liked member of the Tent Club, although he had on one occasion been "fired" from membership for a day.

The macho Jonathan was extremely competitive, an almost compulsive "I'm first"er. His first question after tests had been graded was, "Who got the highest grade?" He was adventuresome. Though he frequently had occasion to rue the day, he often found ingenious ways to defy authority. His most daring escapade was the one of putting paper in the locks of the school doors and piling sand into the window casings, a prank much appreciated by peers if not by the principal. He had guts. Jonathan's mettle was tested early in the year, before the formation of the Tent Club, when Billy played a "game"

34

TABLE 1

Cast of Characters

Winners		*Losers*	
Jonathan:	Role Transcender	Kenny:	Teacher's Little Helper
Billy:	Practitioner of Force	Jason:	Cry-Baby
Chad:	Strategist	Denver:	Sissy
Tommy:	Bookworm	Ronnie:	Braggart
Jeffrey:	"The Professor"	Edward:	Mama's Boy
Derek:	Idea Man		
Paul:	Follower		
Nicky:	Follower		

he called "getting Jonathan." Jonathan might have had a fighting chance against Billy alone but not against Billy supported by other boys who had been bullied into joining him. Jonathan often left the playground with a bruised face or bleeding nose. "But I stuck in there. I just stayed no matter what," he told another boy in a similar situation much later. This was real machismo. So, also, was the way he used his imagination in introducing war-strategy games, which he interested his peers in as an alternative to ball games. This game gained in popularity over the school year and the boys read every book they could find on World War II. With their model tanks, guns, and soldiers they replayed the events they read about. And though Jonathan did not seek leadership in this game, he nevertheless exercised it.

Despite the undeniable machismo—or perhaps being undeniably macho made it possible—Jonathan was gentle and helpful as well. On one occasion when Kenny, obviously fearful of the consequences, was being egged on to fight, Jonathan sensed his fears and gave him advice based on his own experience. Not too proud to confess moments of weakness himself, he told Kenny, "I didn't want to fight either. But you got to. So I'd just get with the big guys and put up my fists and when they charged, I'd charge. Then it looks like you're fighting but you don't have to." The important factor was not whether or not a boy could fight but whether he could convince other boys that he could fight. (This, in a way, was analogous to Chad's "fake-liking": a kind of "fake-fighting.") Although Kenny was an excluded boy and Jonathan a popular member of the Tent Club, Jonathan had been interested enough in Kenny's dilemma to take time out to advise him on how to be macho, how to get along in the male world.

Jonathan also showed sympathy for another loser, Edward. At one time he even circulated a petition among Tent Club boys to permit

Edward to become a member, and only Billy's veto, "over my dead body"—emphasized by tearing up Jonathan's petition into a dozen pieces—prevented Jonathan's kindly gesture from achieving success.

What was most striking about Jonathan was his ability to be openly affectionate with friends. When told once that Chad had said something offensive about him, he threw his arms around Chad and said, "Chad is my friend. I wouldn't do anything to hurt Chaddy." When he and Billy were called into the principal's office after a bloody fight, they were told to shake hands. They did. "Now why don't you give one another a hug?" the principal suggested. Jonathan agreed but Billy could not do such a nonmacho thing. "Never!" said Billy, relenting only when he realized that hugging Jonathan was the only way he would be able to get out of the principal's office.

A final test of Jonathan's strength came on a camping trip when he fell and seriously hurt his leg. His doctor said he would have permanent damage and it would be months before he could run or play ball again. Within weeks Jonathan was running and playing ball. He was not one to be licked.

Billy

Billy was a believer in and a practitioner of *force*. In a word, a bully. If Jonathan had no problem with hugging and the expression of affection, Billy did. There was never any question about Billy's belonging to the Tent Club. In that sense he was a winner. But once the Tent Club had become a reality, his old position as top dog was doomed. In that sense he was, relatively at least, a loser.

Before the Tent Club had been organized long enough to offer a boy group protection, a boy who disagreed with Billy might pay for his mistake with a bloody nose or a black eye. After the formation of the Tent Club, Billy had to fight not only the boy who offended him but also the seven other club members: the Tent Club boys had made an unspoken pledge to support one another against Billy the bully. Although Billy chose not to tackle the overwhelming odds against him, he did not like being merely "one of the gang," and he made numerous attempts to regain his former position as the "big boss."

The peer-group boys did not control Billy by beating him up, as he would have done with them: fighting as a means of showing dominance or maintaining control was no longer used within the group, although it continued to be used against boys outside the group. The Tent Club boys taunted Billy with frequent reminders that there was a weakness in his macho armor: he had been susceptible to Chad's flattery. He had let himself be "used." (There were few taunts more biting than that of "I used you" from the boys and girls of Pine Hill.) Billy's humiliation was painful to watch. He visibly shrank from the words that exposed his vulnerability to flattery. Chad's not-so-secret weapon had been his successful use of "fake-liking," and it contributed to Billy's downfall.

There is a sad ending to Billy's story, for he was never able to accept being merely one of the Tent Club boys. Throughout the fourth grade he fought for control until the Tent Club boys had had enough of him and they turned against him. Billy crumbled. Another class of peers had to be found for him. And, although he lived in the same neighborhood with Jonathan, Tommy, Paul, and Derek, he was never to be their companion again.

Chad

Chad was a *wheeler-dealer*, an operator, a *strategist*. If Jonathan was a winner because he showed nurturance as well as "true grit," and Billy a winner because he could use force, Chad was a winner because he could case all the angles. He was one of the organizers of the Tent Club. He was the artful practitioner of "fake-liking." Fake-liking was something a boy often had to resort to in order to make his way in the male world. Thus, when Chad fake-liked Billy—when Billy was still the "cock of the walk" because of his fighting prowess—he did so to bask in the reflected glory of the high-status Billy. Chad became, in a sense, Billy's public relations man: he boasted of Billy's feats to their peers so that they were constantly reminded of his skill at fighting and at playing Greek dodge ball. He fought for Billy. He cleaned up for him. Eventually he became the major channel of access to Billy himself so that Chad's approval had to be sought by boys who wanted close contact with Billy. Once the Tent Club was formed Chad became a person in his own right.

Jeffrey

In contrast to both Billy and Chad, Jeffrey was neither a fighter nor a manipulator; he was a good student. Being first in the academic arena had always been a sought-after goal of Pine Hill boys and it was here that Jeffrey excelled, with seemingly little effort on his part. His peers called him "The Professor."

Jeffrey did not throw mud balls at any houses, or put paper in the locks of the school's doors, or turn off the lights in the boys' lavatory. He looked on in amusement when other boys took part in the food-throwing battles in the cafeteria, but he did not join them. In fact, he did little that was antiestablishment except to stay outside with his ball team when the teacher told them it was time to go to their classroom, or to continue talking with friends when the teacher told him to be silent.

Jeffrey's research papers were far more extensive in scope than was expected of a third-grade student. He knew all his multiplication and division tables long before they were introduced by the teacher. Because of his outstanding scholarship and ability to finish assigned work ahead of the rest of the class, the teacher often permitted him to spend time reading in the library.

Jeffrey was a valued ball player, but he did not struggle for dominance on the team or within the group. His peers never challenged him to prove himself as a fighter; they knew that this scholarly boy was strong enough to beat any of them. Although only a third-grader, he was able to articulate the goal he was to pursue throughout his school career: to earn top grades and win a commission in a branch of military service that would provide him with an education and economic security.

Jeffrey's obvious intelligence and good manners won him the approval of teachers and parents alike. His peers admired his inner strength and cold disdain for boyish pranks. They called him a "cool" character.

Derek

Derek entered the third grade as an outsider. He had already attended three other schools and was, in effect, "new boy on the block." Like many children new to a school, he was at first uneasy and watchful. He made no effort to speak to any of the boys in the classroom, nor did they approach him. At the end of September his teacher referred to him as "withdrawn" and added, "He doesn't respond to affection at all. When I speak to him he acts as if he doesn't hear me. When he does talk to me or the other children he speaks in a sing-songy voice." When ball games were teacher-directed and every child in the class had to be chosen for one or the other of the two teams, Derek was the last child to be chosen. "Derek is the most rejected child in my class. The children don't like him. He is always chosen last," the teacher commented.

Derek first attempted to establish a relationship with Ronnie, another boy new to the classroom, possibly because he perceived him as being "in the same boat." But Ronnie had his eye on Chad as his ticket to peer acceptance and he would have nothing to do with Derek, who was an outsider and seemed unlikely to gain peer acceptance. When Derek tried to sit beside Ronnie in the cafeteria, he was pushed away with the remark, "Get out of here, I don't want you sitting beside me." After several such rejections Derek abandoned his attempts to make friends with Ronnie and became a loner. It was this characteristic that brought him to the attention of Paul's and Jonathan's mothers. They had noticed him riding his bicycle in lonely circles around the areas where their sons played with their peers, and they decided to intervene. They invited Derek to lunch at their homes on weekends. In this way Paul and Jonathan learned that Derek was an *idea man*. It was Derek who suggested mud-balling the houses and cars in their neighborhood and showed the other boys how it was done. One such escapade met with great success even though the boys were caught and had to spend the rest of the weekend in a massive clean-up effort. By the time the Tent Club was organized Derek had gained enough prestige to be permitted to join.

Tommy

Like Jeffrey, Tommy was an excellent student, even a "book-worm." He was also a slender boy, and one might have predicted that he would be rejected. But this was not the case. Belonging was never a struggle for him. He always seemed to have belonged. His older sister was a brilliant student and—more important to a boy—captain of the school patrols. His father was a Little League coach as well as an influential person in school affairs. But these factors in and of themselves would not have been enough to ensure peer-group acceptance. The fact that he was a Little Leaguer and an aggressive ball player was probably much more of a determinant.

Paul

Paul was a founding father of the Tent Club. It had not been his idea, but he had agreed to it and helped to make it possible. As a *follower*, Paul had enthusiastically accepted the leadership of others and there were few escapades in which he did not take part. Like Jonathan, Paul could show affection, and he often put his arm around a Tent Club boy as they walked side by side on the play-ground. Paul could be counted on to "hang in there" when the other boys needed him.

Nicky

Nicky was readily admitted to the group, for, like Paul, he was a good follower and would participate in any escapade—even to the extent of starting a fire in the wastebasket in his family's recreation room at the urging of peers. Throughout the school year he was the quiet member of the group. Although he never initiated any of their antiestablishment activities, he encouraged the ideas of others. Nicky had been a neighborhood playmate of Jeffrey and Chad's from infancy, and this early, ongoing association probably helped him gain membership in the Tent Club.

Kenny

Kenny was one of the smallest boys in the third grade. He did not particularly like to play ball games, nor did he play particularly well. His teachers had always been a source of comfort and support to him and he clung to them long after other boys had declared their independence. Although any boy concerned with his male image would do anything to avoid the world of girls and women, Kenny helped with housekeeping tasks in the classroom and basked in the teacher's rewards—hugs and loving words—for doing them.

Kenny's third-grade teacher had wanted to prevent any boy in her class from being excluded from the male peer group, but when she began to have problems enforcing her will on the boys she decided to concentrate primarily on Kenny, who had always shown his willingness to cooperate with her. She bestowed leadership and decision-making rights on him. Her interference proved disastrous for him. Until this time Kenny had never shown the slightest interest in Greek dodge ball and did not even know the rules of the game as the children played it. But he was made referee, which meant that he was, in effect, the "boss" of the game and its players. He was proud of the authority invested in him by the teacher as he called the shots. As long as the teacher hovered nearby, Kenny's decisions—right or wrong—were upheld.

But when the teacher walked to another part of the playground, the game was immediately taken over by Billy, who called the shots as he saw them. His authority thus challenged, Kenny ran helplessly from one team member to another insisting that he was the boss. "You have to listen to me," he told them. The teacher returned to the game each time and agreed. "Listen to Kenny. He's the referee. If you don't listen to him I'll take you inside." Passively rejected before, he now became rejected with a vengeance. The boys beat him up.

Kenny again turned to his teacher for comfort and, encouraged by her apparent appreciation, he became a martinet, a watchdog, the "tattletale" of the classroom. It was a profession without honor and it brought him further grief. When the school rules as he knew them were broken, he chided the culprit, recited the rule, and warned, "I'm gonna tell!"

A typical incident: in the cafeteria, third-grader Monica called to her second-grade friend Sandra, "Come on over to my table." As Sandra picked up her lunch and headed for the place Monica had saved for her at the third-grade table, Kenny waved her back. "No, no, you can't. It's against the rules. When you sit down in one place you have to stay there. You can't get up and move." Intimidated by the warning of a third-grade boy, Sandra went back to her table and sat down, but Monica urged, "Come on. Don't listen to Kenny." Sandra and Kenny looked at the lunchroom aide; it seemed clear that she would not interfere. Once more Sandra picked up her tray and headed for Monica's table. Again, Kenny waved her back. "No, no, it's against the rules. Stay there or I'll tell." This time Sandra ignored Kenny. She sat down beside Monica. Kenny was defeated. He had attempted to maintain law and order in the cafeteria whether the adults in charge had wanted it or not. But rather than being reinforced by the cafeteria aide, he had been ignored.

Kenny clung more feverishly than before to the teacher. He insisted that all classroom chores be assigned to him regardless of prior arrangements. The feeding of the fish, for example, was a highly coveted privilege shared by the children on a rotating basis, but now when the hands of the clock reached ten, Kenny dashed for the fish food shouting, "I'll feed the fish!" When papers had to be passed out he dogged his teacher's footsteps, insisting, "I'll pass out the papers!" Kenny's offers of help became all-encompassing demands. "I'll clap the erasers!" "I'll wash the boards!" "I'll clean the paintbrushes!" "I'll get the books!" "I'll take the note to the office!" "I'll run the movie projector!" "I'll get the books!" "I'll take care of the children while you're out of the room!" Ms. North admitted that Kenny was becoming a nuisance. "After getting a lot of attention he wants more. He finds things to do to help me and if I don't want help he persists until I'm ready to go out of my mind." Failing to find acceptance among peers, Kenny had turned to the teacher for ego reinforcement, only to find that she also rejected the excessive demands his offers of help made on her.

Kenny failed another macho test: he did not like to fight and usually would refuse to fight even when challenged. In the spring of the year, for example, he was absent from school for several days. The girls volunteered the information that Kenny had "hurt his leg."

When asked how it happened they explained, "He got beaten up by Paul, Chad, Jonathan, Billy, and Derek." "Why?" I asked. They didn't know. "They just hate him," they said. When I questioned the boys named by the girls, they said that yes, they had done it, but that it had been "accidental." When Kenny returned to school he would not discuss the matter, and when Denver suggested that they get some "guys" together and go after Paul, Chad, Jonathan, Billy, and Derek, Kenny would have nothing to do with the suggestion. Even when obviously hurt he would not fight back.

Jason

Jason violated one of the most fundamental principles of machismo as established by the Pine Hill boys. He cried frequently, and often without apparent reason. The teacher worried about Jason and tried to console him. His peers were not so kind. They attributed his tears to a flaw in his character: he was simply not a man. They summed up the essence of Jason in five words: "Jason is a cry-baby."

Jason enjoyed sitting in the rocking chair in the classroom listening to recordings of songs and stories. He was a gentle child who never forced himself on others. But his gentle, passive behavior seemed to annoy the Tent Club boys and they found ways to be deliberately cruel to him. Once on the playground Jonathan, Derek, and Paul threw him on the ground, sat on him, and ripped his shirt. Jason did not mention the incident to the teacher, but she noticed his torn shirt and asked how it happened. Jason shrugged his shoulders and said, "It's okay." He even told the boys who had been responsible that he didn't mind.

Jason did show anger and aggression on occasion, but it was always directed toward the two boys with whom he spent most of his free play time: Kenny and Denver. Once when their arguments got out of hand and threatened to create a problem in the classroom, the teacher sent all three boys to the office to talk to the principal. Jason became so hysterical that he could not speak coherently. When he was calm he told the principal that he was afraid that the office would call his mother and that his family would be ashamed of him. Jason was obsessively afraid of disgracing his family in some way. He was afraid of calling attention to himself.

Denver

Denver liked girls and the girls liked Denver. The peer-group boys said that Denver was a "sissy." He was a good ball player and his father served as the substitute coach for the Little League team on which some of the peer-group boys played. But Denver's skill as a ball player was not enough to offset his violation of the most fundamental rule of machismo: do not be like or play with girls. His association with girls was reason enough to reject Denver from membership in the Tent Club.

At one time or another Denver was the special love interest of each and every girl in the third grade. They chased him on the playground. He was kissed more often than any other third-grade boy. The girls sang about love and marriage with Denver, chanting, for example, "Denver and Michelle sitting in a tree, K-I-S-S-I-N-G. First comes love, then comes marriage, then comes Denver with the baby carriage." None of this embarrassed him. He loved the teasing and he loved the girls. He named Michelle, Elizabeth, and Megan as some of his best friends.

But Denver also wanted peer-group acceptance as much as any boy, and it wasn't forthcoming. "No one likes Denver except Megan Moore," Jonathan said to explain why Denver had been excluded from the Tent Club. I turned to Denver, who was standing nearby and had heard Jonathan's remark, and asked, "Is Megan your girlfriend?" Denver did not answer. In the face of this kind of peer disapproval he was silent. Jonathan answered for him, "Yeah, they sit together all the time. He's just a sissy." "Do you have a girlfriend?" I asked Jonathan and Chad. "Yecch!" was their answer.

When the boys were in the fourth grade they indicated that Denver had failed other machismo tests given him by the peer-group boys. "We asked him this real easy word and he couldn't even read it," they said. In this case it had been a literacy test that Denver had failed. And there were indications of other kinds of tests. "Denver likes to talk about drag racing and we like to play ball and war strategy games," they said. The boys often called him "dummy" because of his poor performance in the classroom. But the primary reason for Denver's exclusion from peer-group membership was his excessively close ties to girls.

Ronnie

Ronnie had many strong macho characteristics—he was aggressive, a good fighter, he played ball well—but on the minus side, he made exaggerated claims about his ability in all these areas. He bragged that he was the best fighter, the best ball player, the best at almost everything real men do. The in-group boys responded by ignoring him.

Ronnie was a new boy in the class. As we know, he had brushed aside Derek's overtures of friendship to seek friendship with Chad, the gateway to Billy. In November Ronnie threw his arm around Chad's shoulders and announced to the entire class, "Chad is my best friend, aren't you Chad?" Chad nodded very slightly, for he was a boy who played the odds, and the final decision was not yet in on Ronnie. For the remainder of the month Ronnie followed in Chad's footsteps. He spoke to everyone of his close friendship with Chad as though it were a proven fact. However, Ronnie's friendship with Chad was short-lived, for when he asked to join the Tent Club, he was told they already had more members than they could handle.

Soon after the Tent Club was organized, its members met to demonstrate, as much to themselves as to others, their new relationship and to "make up secrets" that only members could share. Ronnie hovered nearby, watching closely. Then, without warning or apparent reason, he began to hit a fourth-grade girl. Before an adult could reach him, he had thrown the girl against the brick wall of the school hard enough to cause a large knot to appear on her forehead. When asked for an explanation, he said, "I don't know why I did it." He added that he was not sorry and would not apologize to the girl. Later that day Ronnie was sent to the office for hitting another girl, Michelle. "Why did you hit Michelle?" the teacher wanted to know. He was already in trouble. Did he want to get sent home from school? With his eyes riveted to the floor, Ronnie said, "She kept bugging me to beat up Denver." "So you beat up Michelle instead?" the teacher asked. "I just can't understand what happened to Ronnie today. He's been so good this past month," the teacher said.

Ronnie's attack on the two girls might have been his way of trying to convince the peer-group boys that they had made a mistake; that he was a real man; that he rejected girls and women to the extent that he beat up on them. But excluding the girls from the rough games of boys was for their own good, and it was this part of the macho code that Ronnie failed to understand. There were no macho points given to a boy for "beating up" a girl.

Ronnie was far more insistent on gaining peer approval than was Denver, Kenny, or Jason. It seemed a matter of life and death to him. When all his attempts met with failure, he shunned every child in his classroom and turned instead to Carrie, a second-grade cousin with whom he had grown up. He ate lunch with her and played with her on the playground. Several times a day Ronnie would petition the teacher to permit him to go to Carrie's room because "I have something to tell her." This relationship lasted until late February, when concerned teachers and parents decided that the two children might be playing "doctor" after school, and that this was unhealthy for both of them. With the loss of Carrie, Ronnie began to spend time with Denver, Kenny, and Jason.

One more incident should receive some attention before we leave Ronnie's story. The last time I saw him as a third-grader was when I stopped in the classroom to say goodbye for the summer. Ronnie ran to me and said, "You like me better than anyone, don't you Ms. Best?" "How did you know, Ronnie?" I asked. In a triumphant voice he said to his classmates, "See, she likes me better than anybody." On the last day of school Ronnie was playing the old "I'm first" game, and no one was interested. The talk was of summer plans, and they did not include Ronnie.

Edward

Edward entered Pine Hill late in the third-grade year, so that he has not yet played a part in the saga of the peer group. He was an excellent student. Because of a series of operations to correct a hearing loss, he had spent far more time with adults and in home-tutoring classes than he had with peers and in school. He dressed impeccably, in a suit complete with a white shirt and tie. It was hardly proper attire for sports, but then Edward neither cared for nor was good at playing games of any kind. When he had a problem he asked for help from the teacher but never from peers. This was a tactical error in his quest for peer acceptance. It seemed to the boys in the class that Edward was on the side of the establishment.

Without any basis for their assumption—except for the way he dressed and the manner in which he behaved toward adults—the peer-group boys decided that Edward had come from a "hoity-toity" school, where students were always perfect. "Look at us," Jonathan said. "We do things we shouldn't do sometimes and we get into trouble. But not him. He's so-o-o good." Being too good, trying to fit into the establishment rather than declaring independence from it by engaging in minor pranks, was not macho. This behavior won him praise from the teacher but disapproval from peers. Would a really manly boy be so good? The in-boys did not think so.

But Edward's worst offense was to violate the most fundamental tenet of the boys' world: he brought his *mother*—a female—in. This was a fatal mistake. Having to tolerate the interference of teachers in their disputes and girls in their ball games was bad enough. But *mothers*? A mother did not belong in the world the macho boys had established for themselves at school—a world free of parental controls, governed by their own rules.[1] Edward's mother was frequently at school and she often did volunteer work in their classroom. The boys minded her presence in their world and they strongly resented her interference in their affairs.

Edward, like all new boys, had to be tested for evidence of machismo. The boys teased him whenever they could do so without being seen. Billy, in particular, tested him in this way. But, unlike Jonathan, who "stayed in there" whatever the punishment, Edward, apparently unaware that he was being tested, cried or complained and ran to his mother for comfort whenever she was in the classroom. Perhaps because he had entered the class so late in the school year, the boys deferred their final judgment of Edward until the fourth grade. Then the testing continued. On one occasion, for example, the boys and girls were standing in line as preparation for going to the library when Billy poked Edward and said something under his breath. Edward immediately complained to the teacher that Billy was being mean to him again. "Edward can't take it," the peer-group boys explained to me when they saw me watching the exchange between Edward, Billy, and the teacher. "The other day Billy called Edward a name and then Edward called Billy a name so Billy hit him and Edward wasn't even crying." Then, according to Jonathan, Edward saw his mother and ran to her. "He started to cry, 'Mama, Mama!' when he wasn't even hurt." Chad said contemptously, "He's just a baby. He can't take it." The other boys agreed.

There was no place in a macho world for a boy who cried when he "wasn't even hurt" and who, in addition, ran to his mother to complain. Her protests to the teacher and to the parents of the boys resulted in punishment for the boys in the form of loss of play time. Edward's mother thus protected him from the macho tests of the peer group.

·4·

SOME CONSEQUENCES
OF REJECTION

In the not too distant future . . . as research in social psychology influences reading teachers, we may see some modifications of the remedial process. Teachers may better analyze and understand . . . the pupil's interactions with the peer group and its effects on him. . . . Moreover, they will realize that the pupil's growth in reading may progress only in proportion to the supportive and reinforcing effects provided by the teacher *and the peer group.*[1]

At Pine Hill reading ability was one determinant of peer associations. Among the first-graders, learning to read was what going to school was all about, and the importance of success in this *rite de passage* can hardly be overestimated. One time when the mother of a first-grader asked him what he had done in school that day, he replied, "We didn't do anything. We didn't read." When the time came for the first-grade children to graduate from the "readiness" stage to first-grade readers, all were not equally ready, and it did not take those children reading in hardback books long to make judgments about the others. Those still in "readiness" came to be labeled as "dumb," the group reading hardback books as "smart." With the exception of the first-grader Adam (discussed in chapter 6), the boys who found themselves without playmates were also the boys having initial reading difficulties. "They don't get chosen in games as often as some of the others," said Ms. Carter. And Ms. Minor commented, "I could put my reading groups together just by watching the boys who chose other boys as friends. They know who is like them and who isn't."

In the third grade, reading ability continued to be a definitive factor in group membership. Of the six boys who entered third grade with reading skills below grade level—all of whom were in the normal range of test intelligence and should have been able to reach and maintain group level—two ended at about grade level or above, and three fell behind. It did, indeed, seem true, as Sarane Boocock noted, that "what goes on in schools and what seems to matter most to a student's level of accomplishment is who he interacts with there."[2]

The inevitable question is: were boys rejected by peers because they did not read well, or were they poor readers because they had been rejected? At Pine Hill the answer was: sometimes the first, sometimes the second.

A year after the Tent Club was organized the Tent Club boys were asked why some boys had not been admitted to membership, and the reply indicated that some kind of literacy test had been involved. We recall that Denver had failed the test by not being able to pronounce "a real easy word like 'it' or 'the' or something like that," according to Derek. Though clearly an exaggeration of Denver's reading disability, Derek's comment showed that there were fairly specific tests that had to be passed in order to gain admission, and one of these was a reading test.

Table 2 shows what effect being excluded from the peer group had on reading ability. Each boy's achievement status at the end of the third grade, based on a comparison of that year's fall and spring reading scores, is shown in relation to his group status (that is, his membership status in the Tent Club). The abbreviations BC and WC next to the boys' names indicate whether their fathers were blue-collar or white-collar workers.

Among the first- and second-graders it seemed that reading ability might have been a factor in determining a boy's popularity with his peer group. In the third grade, high reading ability seemed to be not so much a prerequisite for peer-group acceptance as a consequence. And because of this apparent impact of group status on learning to read it became important to trace the processes by which peer relations affected learning.

It is far easier to describe the alienating process than it is to explain it. Despite the considerable amount of research on the relationship between group membership and learning ability, there has not been a great deal of theorizing on the subject. David C. Epperson is one of the few researchers who have offered suggestions. Based on a study of 753 pupils in grades three through twelve, he proposes an alienation theory: "peers . . . exclude academically and socially incompetent pupils," and such exclusion by peers results in a feeling of both "task and social powerlessness in the excluded."[3] Exclusion from the group leads a child to engage in diversionary and energy-consuming activities in order to gain acceptance. Such activity, in turn, makes him less acceptable to his peers, and so on.

> . . . much psychological energy is likely to be consumed by behaviors aimed at gaining needed support or in compensating for the

TABLE 2

Group and Achievement Status of Third-Grade Boys

Name and Father's Occupational Status	Group Status	Fall Score	Spring Score	Achievement Status
Nicky (BC)	In all year	no score	3.9	Improved
Jeffrey (BC)	In all year	4.1	5.5	Improved
Jonathan (WC)	In all year	4.8	8.8	Improved
Chad (BC)	In all year	2.3	3.5	Improved
Paul (WC)	In all year	4.6	5.1	Improved
Tommy (WC)	In all year	4.5	5.5	Improved
Billy (WC)	In all year	no score	7.8	Improved
Derek (WC)	Admitted during year	2.0	4.2	Improved
Ronnie (BC)	Out all year	2.2	2.2	No improvement
Denver (BC)	Out all year	2.6	2.2	Declined
Kenny (BC)	Out all year	2.8	2.3	Declined
Jason (BC)	Out all year	2.7	2.3	Declined

deficiency. To achieve the needed support, an acceptable level of performance on classroom tasks is required that suggests the circular nature of the process. First the pupil is not supported, which precipitates energy-consuming processes that leave less energy available for classroom tasks. This leads to lower performance on the tasks, making him less acceptable to others in the class, hence he gains less support. Over a period of time this circular process influences whether or not he can approach actualizing his potential. When such a circular process occurs, the pupil is likely to develop a cognitive orientation towards others in the classroom which can be conceptualized as alienation.[4]

At Pine Hill there was, indeed, evidence of the diversionary activities Epperson refers to , activities designed to prove male competence in the nonacademic spheres of the macho world since they could not show superiority in the academic—reading—area. In all the primary grades there were boys who disrupted classroom lessons to demonstrate their willingness to defy the establishment. In the third grade these energy-consuming activities included clowning for the benefit of peers rather than working on assignments, bragging about superior fighting ability, and escaping from the classroom for long periods of time to make contacts in the boys' lavatory. In the allocation of energy, a minimum was assigned to school tasks. Learning to read took second place to gaining a foothold in the peer world. Some of this dysfunctional allocation of the child's resources was also evidence of his ability to read the group's code.

When it had become clear to Ronnie, Kenny, Denver, and Jason that they were out, they no longer put forth even the minimum effort required to learn to read. Activities to achieve both task competence and social competence, as delineated by Epperson, waned. They gave up trying to learn to read. They even gave up trying to be accepted. About a month after the Tent Club had been organized, Ronnie, in response to nothing at all, suddenly remarked as if in protest to his teacher, "I did my best." He was clearly not referring to his school work.

In March, the teacher commented that the school year was already over for Ronnie, Denver, and Kenny. "They won't do a thing I ask them to do. They just pretend not to hear or they tell me not to worry about it."

Ronnie's and Kenny's loss of motivation expressed itself in their insistence that they didn't have to learn to read and that they didn't mean to. "I'm not going to do this!" cried Kenny about his reading assignment. "I don't have to learn to read. I'm gonna be a fireman like my father when I grow up and he doesn't read either!" He refused to try. "I don't have to read to be a fireman when I grow up!" Similarly, when the teacher expressed concern over Ronnie's refusal to do his school work, he said, "Don't worry about me. I'll get a job when I grow up. I don't have to learn to read. I'll get a job with Benny May's [a road construction company] so just don't worry about it." His teacher shook her head. "It's all over for Ronnie." As far as motivation was concerned, it was.

The concern of the rejected boys themselves was far less with their academic progress, or lack of it, than with their inability to achieve acceptance in their peer world. They knew intuitively what Asher, Oden, and Gottman had found, namely that "the consequences of low peer acceptance may be more severe than the consequences of low achievement."[5] The consequences of low peer acceptance may indeed be severe.

The under-researched six- to eight-year-olds look so young, so little, so innocent, so fresh that it is hard to take them seriously. Ten years later many parents and teachers will be horrified to learn that it is *their* child, *their* pupil who has been making bombs for fun, drag-racing, or selling drugs. They will attribute the behavior to puberty, to adolescence, to the mass media, to disturbed family relations, to lack of a secure role, to unemployment, to false values, to parental permissiveness, to a host of other quite reasonable and persuasive factors. All, no doubt, correct in specific instances.

> In Montgomery County, [Maryland], where 100,000 homes line the suburban streets, an increasingly popular pastime among teenagers these days is making explosives and blowing things up. Since last November, homemade bombs have shattered three cars, blown out a backyard, set fire to an elementary school shed, and ripped apart at least five mailboxes in the county. "The most fun part about it," observed a 17-year-old whose targets have been limited to mailboxes, "is seeing it happen, seeing something destroyed like that . . ."[6]

The excluded boys I was observing at Pine Hill are probably not going to become delinquents or criminals. No one knows what they are going to become. But by the time they ended the third grade there were already indications that something was wrong. They were stealing, they were throwing stones at men in trains, they were killing birds and fish for fun.

Hostility. Kenny, the teacher's little helper, now stopped insisting on helping. He was angry. When I playfully punched him on the arm, he snapped back at me: "If you ever do that again I'm going to report you to the principal. I'll have my father sue you!" That was one way of getting back at the world.

Stealing. Toward the end of January a sixth-grade patrol reported to his teacher that Jason had given him a Kennedy half-dollar. The teacher investigated and found that many other children had also been given Kennedy half-dollars. He collected the money and approached Jason. Where had the money come from? Why had he given it to the children? The boy denied he had given the coins to the children. He had never even seen them before. Finally, sobbing violently, he said he had "found them" at home in his parents' drawer.

Killing fish. In the third grade when Denver, whose first- and second-grade teachers had spoken of him as a "sweet child," found that he was not to be invited to be a member of the Tent Club, he ripped a fingernail from Nina's hand. By January his many temperamental outbursts required that he be isolated from the class to calm down. "Denver," said his teacher, "has become mean. He was never mean before." One day in February while the children and their teacher were eating lunch, he asked to be excused to go to the lavatory but went instead to his classroom. There he broke the heating equipment on the fish tank. When he was asked why, the boy who had once been characterized as a sweet child replied, "I wanted to see the fish freeze to death."

Killing birds. When Ronnie was sure he was out of the Tent Club and that there was no point in trying for membership, he began to hit girls in the school and to fight with Kenny, Denver, Jason, and second-grade boys. He was frequently sent to the principal's bench to "cool off." He bragged about his skill in fighting and he bragged about behaving maliciously. "Yesterday my friend and me threw stones at pigeons and we killed one of them. It was just like a moving picture, man! We go to the railroad tracks and throw stones at trains, too. Once a man looked out and we threw stones at him and hit him. Man, that was fun!"

Larry: Lost and Found

In view of the frightening consequences of group rejection for personality development as well as for learning, the question inevitably arose: can the harm be undone? Can adult intervention save a boy who has suffered such traumatic experiences? Until we learned how to prevent peer rejection, or at least how to mollify its consequences, were there ways to help a boy retrace his steps? The story of Larry shows that it may be possible. Under certain circumstances the Epperson cycle could be broken and the alienation process reversed.

The schoolboy's world may not have as many circles as Dante's

Hell, but it is difficult to imagine a fate worse than being relegated to the "SLD" (Specific Learning Disability) classes. To be sent into that realm was, in the vivid and accurate words of one who had suffered that disgrace, to be dumped in the trash can. Reclaiming these boys—there were very few girls in these classes—was next to impossible. Larry was one exception.

Larry came to school from a home that had many skeletons in the closet, a hostile home full of fierce ethnic prejudices that were already part of his mental baggage when he entered school. He came to the SLD class at Pine Hill in his fifth school year, so I had no direct contact with him before that time. But from the first grade on, he had a record of frequent angry outbursts against others, which set in motion Epperson's circular process: frequent rejections by peers as early as the first grade, resulting, as Epperson found in his subjects, in a sense of both "social powerlessness" and "task powerlessness." Predictably, he was a nonreader.

The school psychologist found Larry to be of average intelligence, especially verbal, and extremely hostile. I was challenged to see if the alienation process could be reversed, if "task power" could generate "social power" and thus break the Epperson process. Fortunately, as it turned out, there was a strong motivational factor that I could use. He had only recently moved into a new neighborhood, and since he did not attend the same school the other boys did, he had told them that he went to a "special school" but would join them next year in junior high school. He had been able to make friends with the neighborhood boys. It was his first experience at being included in a boys' group and he wanted desperately to remain in it. He knew he had not told his new friends the truth. He was not scheduled to go to their junior high the following year but was to be transferred to a special education class in another junior high, Greenwood. "I told the kids in my neighborhood I was going to Spring Lake next year. If I go to Greenwood and don't go to Spring Lake, how can I ever face them again? What are they going to think of me?" If he could make it into the regular sixth-grade class at Pine Hill before the end of the sixth grade, he could go to Spring Lake. This proved to be a powerful incentive.

Our first meeting was disappointing. Larry glared at me from his chair. At our second meeting he spoke, but his words were hostile. "Don't you know I can't read those words?" he snarled when I suggested playing a word game. But little by little his confidence in me grew until he looked forward to our sessions together. When I was not there he would ask, "Did I forget you yesterday or did you forget me?" Then one day the story of his desperate ploy with the neighborhood boys burst forth as from an erupting volcano. He wanted to be a "regular" guy in a "regular" classroom so that he could go to junior high with his neighborhood friends.

"I see those boys in the sixth-grade class and I know they're not like the kids in my class." He knew that he and his classmates were rejects. He did not want to be one. We explored ways of getting him into a "regular" class with "regular" guys so that he could continue to face his friends, so that he would not again be rejected by a group of his peers. He would, of course, have to learn to read and to control his temper before we could approach the school principal and present his petition.

First, the tantrums. Why? "I don't know how to put this into words so it sounds right," he began, "but when the teacher gives me a paper like that"—and from his pocket he pulled a paper with six pictures and six spaces for spelling the words—"I get mad and then I make mistakes." See, I misspelled s-t-a-r, and I know how to spell that word but I just get so mad I don't know what I'm doing." His message came through loud and clear. He was angry because he felt the work assigned him was more appropriate for first-graders than for a sixth-grade boy. It labeled him dumb; in brief, it was a put-down and to be put down made him furious. He had had frequent experiences with put-downs and, knowing no other way to deal with them, he had tantrums. Now that we understood, could he control his temper while he learned to read? He'd try. There were no more tantrums. His improvement in reading was dramatic. He went into the regular sixth grade for social studies and I soon felt confident enough to approach the principal with a request to have him officially transferred to the regular sixth-grade class. He agreed.

But Larry's mother was skeptical, and he, bitter. "See her?" he said, bursting into tears for the first time since I had known him. "She just wants me in Greenwood. No one is going to do anything for me. I'm going to get thrown into the trash can again." His mother's attitude made his efforts seem hopeless. His tears turned to heavy sobbing. I sent for the principal, who came at once and took Larry's face into his hands. "I want you to look at me, Larry, so you will know I'm telling the truth. You have to trust some adults to help you make the right decision for you. Larry, your mom stopped in the office a few minutes ago and for the first time in two years I saw her smile. I never saw her smile last year but today she smiles. She thinks her son is happy and is making progress that she can see. She's very proud of you. I want to ask you three questions. First. Do you like Ms. Jackson's class?" "Yes." "Why?" "Because I like it here at Pine Hill." "Second. Do you like being in Mr. Packard's class?" "Yes." "Why?" "Because I like the kids and I get along with them."

"Third. Do you like working with Ms. Best?" "Yes." "Why?" "Because she's trying to help me." "Are you saying that you want to stay here at Pine Hill?" "Yes." "Why?" "Because I like it here." "Good enough. If you want to be in a regular classroom here at Pine Hill I will support you in that." Considerably cheered but still suspicious, Larry asked, "Hasn't my behavior been all right? I haven't done anything." "I have no argument with your behavior Larry. There was only one incident this year, and otherwise you've been fine."

Larry went into the regular sixth-grade class at Pine Hill. At the end of the school year he scored slightly above grade level in reading on national tests. The following school year he went to Spring Lake Junior High School with his neighborhood friends. Reports from his school showed that he was doing well academically and that he seemed to be getting along well with his peers.

PART TWO

The Second Curriculum: Gender-Role Socialization

·5·

WHAT WAS BEING TAUGHT

> She's made of sunshine, sugar, and spice
> She'll be pert and pretty and awfully nice
> Someday she's bound to change her name
> Now choose the one that will stay the same.
>
> The name that polls the winning vote
> The famous name that makes up quotes
> The name that thousands . . . (do) employ
> May be the name you name your boy.[1]

In the spring of 1973, as in the spring of each year, the soon-to-be five-year-olds came to kindergarten "Roundup" at Pine Hill to register for the fall term. For this special occasion the girls were wearing frilly dresses and polished Mary Jane shoes and had carefully curled hair. They walked proudly and rewarded adults who praised them for their appearance with pleased smiles. "I got this dress for Easter," said one little girl to the teacher who interviewed her. Little boys in long pants, shirts with collars, and, often, bow ties, tried hard to appear manly and masterful. "I'm exceptionally bright," said one of them to the teacher who was interviewing him. This Roundup was designed to enroll the boys and girls in the official standard curriculum offered by the school: reading, writing, and arithmetic. Actually, it was enrolling them at the same time in another unofficial, unacknowledged, and in many ways more powerful second curriculum, namely one having to do with sex-role socialization. The children's behavior, introductory remarks, and gender-identifiable clothing showed how well prepared they already were.

It was, however, the academic curriculum that generated the most concern among the parents of the kindergarten children. The most frequently asked question was, "When will my child learn to read?" No parent was ever heard to ask, "What will my child read?" or "How will the curriculum materials used at Pine Hill affect how my child feels about himself/herself?" Nor did the teachers ask such questions. It was not that they did not care about the children, but in

1973 they did not know that there could or should be changes in the ways boys and girls were socialized into their sex roles.

Pictures, posters, library books, and textbooks were all-encompassing media for teaching the second curriculum. Teachers, who were themselves victims of the second curriculum, were pivotal in the process of indoctrination. The way sex roles were portrayed and taught seemed to them perfectly suited to the school's program. They believed that boys and girls should be dealt with differently for their own good. "I want my girls to be girls and my boys, boys," said a fourth-grade teacher. A legitimate goal, but then she went on to add, "I don't want them doing the same things or playing the same games. I don't want them dressing alike either!" When I explained why I wanted to change the sexist attitudes and behavior of the children in her classroom, she resisted. She feared that once the children were free to decide their own course they would reverse roles. The specter of boys in dresses and girls bruising their knees on the ball field was too much for her.

The power of the teacher in carrying out the lessons of the second curriculum was exerted in a variety of ways. It was through her, for example, that the boys and girls learned what kind of toys and games were for boys and what kind for girls. In kindergarten the teacher encouraged girls to play in the doll house, but no boy ever played there. Wheeled toys and building equipment like Lego blocks and erector sets were routinely assigned to boys but not to girls. On one occasion the kindergarten teacher asked the principal for more building equipment and wheeled toys. "The girls have enough things to play with in the doll house, but the boys need more building equipment and wheeled toys," she said. When I suggested to the principal that the boys might like to play in the doll house too and that they might also learn something from the experience, he agreed but said he could do nothing about the situation. "If I encourage boys to play in the doll house, the community will run me out."

The boys and girls also learned from the teacher what kind of play equipment was sex-appropriate for them and how much of the playground space they would be permitted for their separate games. Thus, in every classroom when it was time for recess, the boys jumped from their desks and ran to the shelf that held the balls and jump ropes to claim possession of the balls. Their right to seize possession of the balls went undisputed by the teacher, as did their right to most of the playground space. Girls were allowed the jump ropes. Jumping rope and playing hopscotch did not require the large play areas; those games could be played on the sidewalks and fringe areas the boys did not want. The teachers saw nothing remarkable about this. But little girls, seeing boys in the center of the action, could have little doubt that the teachers considered boys and boys' games more important than girls and girls' games. This persistent theme—more space for boys, less space for girls—unchallenged by any teacher, corroborated the girls' view of themselves as inferior and supported the boy's image of themselves as superior and important.

But the teacher's part in conveying the lessons of the second curriculum took an even more direct form in her differential relationships with the boys and girls. The contacts with the girls were more intimate than those with the boys and lasted longer. Thus, for example, when the boys eagerly ran outside to play, the girls fought among themselves for the "privilege" of staying indoors and helping the teacher. This was the time used by teachers to tidy up the classroom, and the girls could help. They did such "feminine" tasks as clapping erasers, cleaning art corners and sinks, and straightening up bookcases and cupboards. The teacher rewarded the girls by praising them lavishly and admitting that she didn't know what she'd do without them. Many girls even arranged to stay at school after dismissal time to help the teacher and receive loving praise, hugs, and, more often than not, a coke or candy bar as well. Even as girls grew older and best friends became more important in their lives than teachers, they never completely gave up the chance to earn rewards for their "feminine" services in the classroom.

As a result of the closer ties the girls maintained with their teachers, they not only had a kind of apprenticeship training in the female role, but they also received greater protection from the teacher than the boys did, even when they had broken a school rule. On one occasion, for example, the third-grade teacher found two of her students, Elizabeth and Denver, sitting on a bench outside the principal's office as punishment for creating a disturbance in the cafeteria. She moved immediately to comfort Elizabeth. "Don't worry, Elizabeth, I'll take care of you," she said soothingly as she put her arms around the crying girl. Then she turned to the boy and asked, "What did you do, Denver?" implying that he was responsible for the situation. Taking Elizabeth by the hand, the teacher led her to the office, where she explained that Elizabeth was a "good girl" and that she had not meant to disobey school rules. She asked that Elizabeth be excused from sitting on the bench and having to explain to the principal what she had done. Still holding Elizabeth by the hand, she led the smiling girl back to the classroom, while Denver was left on the bench to await his fate with the principal. The lesson was indirect but clear: girls, being weak, could expect mercy; boys were strong enough for justice.

The second curriculum was so pervasive throughout the school, so taken for granted, that it would require a major upheaval just to make people aware of it. Even before the children could read the words in books, they could read the messages in book illustrations and pictures on bulletin boards that portrayed women cooking, sewing, and caring for children and men working as firemen, policemen, farmers, postmen, and doctors.

When the children began to read, the pictures were powerfully reinforced by words. The second curriculum depicted boys as aggressive, heroic, imaginative, adventurous, clever, independent, and excellent problem-solvers; girls were shown as inferior, passive, dependent, fearful, bored, lonely, and domestic. The second curriculum showed graphically and verbally in great detail that the differences between boys and girls determined what they could and could not do. A book in the easy-to-read section of the library taught the children that: "Boys eat, girls cook; boys fix things, girls need things fixed; boys invent things, girls use what boys invent; boys build houses, girls keep houses."[2] Boys shown in firefighters' regalia played in scaled-down fire engines; they hiked with a Cub Scout troop, dressed in Tarzan-style leopard skins, and lifted barbells to show how strong they were. Girls were shown playing with dolls, cooking over a campfire with their Brownie troop, and ice skating.

The second curriculum also provided the information that boys were the norm against which girls were to be judged and measured. In a book on psychology, the children learned that "Boys are usually bigger and stronger than girls. This means that boys can do some things that girls cannot do. Girls are usually just as smart as boys."[3] The implication here, that all boys were smart while only some girls were as smart as boys, was readily discerned by Pine Hill children. Although contrary to their own observations that in all grades the children who experienced difficulty in learning to read were boys, this idea was so seductive that there was no resisting it. One took this kind of "science" on faith; one did not test it against one's own experience. If the books said boys were superior to girls, then, of course, boys *were* superior, no matter what the children saw around them.

Great as was the disparity between what the second curriculum taught the boys and girls they were like and what they could actually do, the contrast in career choices presented to them was even greater. In the easy-to-read book mentioned above, girls were offered no more than a supportive function vis-à-vis boys' careers: "boys are doctors: girls are nurses; boys are policemen: girls are metermaids; boys are football players: girls are cheerleaders; boys are Presidents: girls are First Ladies."[4] Other books taught:

A little boy can be a fireman, a baseball player, a bus driver, a policeman, a cowboy, a sailor, a clown, a zoo-keeper, an actor or at the culmination of his career: "An astronaut who lives in a space station and someday grows up to be President of the Nation."[5]

A girl can be a nurse, a stewardess, ballerina, candy shop owner, model, star, secretary, artist, teacher in a nursery school, singer, designer of dresses, bride, or at the peak of her career: "A housewife someday when I am grown and a mother with some children of my own."[6]

The range of career choices offered to boys was limitless; the choices offered to girls were narrow and restricted. At Pine Hill a set of career-education booklets offered over eighty-two options to boys, while girls were given eighteen. The second-curriculum message that boys were superior to girls and could thus make a special contribution to society through their chosen professions was strengthened by the biography section of the library, which offered children four hundred and twelve biographies of famous men and thirty-one of famous women, ten of whom had gained prominence by marrying men who became presidents of the United States.

Textbooks used in grades four through six provided graphic illustrations of men's salaries at various job levels. The total omission of women's income or job status left the impression that the work women did was of questionable monetary value. Thus, the same curriculum materials that taught boys "the sky's the limit" had a different message for girls. Their place was in the home scrubbing and sewing and caring for the children. If they had to work to supplement their husbands' incomes, they could be beauticians, supermarket cashiers, dressmakers, florists, office workers, weavers, or children's librarians, for example.

In addition to labeling women as inferior and fit only for jobs that supported men, the second curriculum made it abundantly clear that girls were expected to "get a husband," become a mother, and be domestic. A favorite tale of Pine Hill's primary-age children, possibly because of the mild defiance of adult authority implied in the story, was Whistle, Mary, Whistle. Mary refuses to whistle for her mother even when she offers her a cow, a pig, a sheep, a trout, a rabbit, a goat, a daisy, a pickle, some honey, bread, a pie, some gold, and even the moon. When Mary's mother offers her the pièce-de-résistance, a man, Mary whistles, "Tweet, tweet, tweet, tweet, I just found out I can."[7]

When I asked the first-grade boys if they would whistle to "get a girl," Michael told me that he thought I had lost my mind. "No way!"

and "Never!" other boys answered. They said, however, that they would whistle for the gold or the moon, and if they couldn't get the gold or the moon, they would settle for the pie or the rabbit.

Career Choices of Boys

In the first grade the social studies unit used a book called *Home and Community Helpers*. It emphasized, as the title indicated, the helping nature of the adult occupations offered. Understandably, therefore, the career choices of the boys indicated a desire to help others. The following stories, written by eight first-grade boys and representative of the group, illustrate the point.

POLICEMAN A policeman helps people
That are in trouble.—By Adam

POLICEMAN I want to be a policeman.
I want to help people with the stop lights.
I want to stop traffic.—By Michael

POLICEMAN Policeman, "Help!"
"Help!" said the clerk.
"Here is help!" I would say.—By Craig

POSTMAN I want to be a postman.
I want to bring people their mail.
I want to read my mail.—By Scott

FIREMAN I want to put out fires.
I want to help people.—By Richard

FIREMAN I want to be a fireman.
I want to put out fires.
I want to help people who are in trouble.
I want to help people who need help.—By Ryan

POLICEMAN I want to be a policeman.
I want to help people.—By Kevin

FARMER I want to feed my people.
I want to milk the cows.
I want to give them food.—By Benny

Although, according to the stereotypes, helping was a characteristic more appropriate to girls than to boys, the boys already knew that the kind of help they offered—firefighting, raising livestock, and fighting crime, for example—was definitely in the macho tradition.

In addition it would earn them significant social and monetary rewards: it would put them "in charge."

The career-education booklets used by second-grade teachers increased the four male choices offered in the first-grade booklets to
over eighty jobs and professions. The boys were thus stimulated to
think on a wider scale, in terms of a bigger, less confined world. This
was a big jump and they took advantage of it. It was not only the
range of job possibilities that was expanded but also the motives for
choosing them. The helping motif remained, but now the booklets
introduced the ideas of liking the work itself and, the most macho
motive of all, making "lots of money." On an interest inventory that
asked the second-grade boys what they wanted to be when they grew
up, they said: "A doctor because I want to help people" (Matthew);
"A doctor because I like to help people" (Ramon); "A doctor because
I like to help people" (John); "A fairman [a person who works at
county fairs]. I like to go to the fairs" (Curtis); "An actor because I
like it" (Cliff); "An IBM technician because they make a lot of
money" (Brian); "A football player so I can make a lot of money"
(Joshua); "A pro football player because I would make a lot of
money" (Brent). George's choice—to be a farmer—was a holdover
from first grade. The child whose answer was the greatest surprise
was Claude, who said, simply, that he wanted to be "A daddy because I like it." The teachings of the second curriculum hadn't yet
registered with him.

In the third grade the second curriculum had no special unit but
used the print media, the visual media, parents, and teachers to
propel the boys into new areas of thinking about careers. Now their
choices reflected the world they had seen outside as well as inside
the classroom. With no textbook restrictions on their choices, fun
and adventure became strong motives. So, in addition to the old
standbys—fireman, policeman, and doctor, there were some new
choices that reflected rather imaginative interests: "A metroliner
comptroller because I like trains" (Jonathan); "A spy chief. I like to
spy" (Paul); "A construction worker. I like to build things" (Derek);
"A motorcycle racer. It is fun" (Nicky); "A professional football
player because I like to play a lot of football" (Tommy); "An airplane
fighter because I like to fight" (Billy); "A robber. I would shoot people and take their money" (Ronnie); "A fireman because . . ." (Jason);
"A doctor to help people" (Kenny).

This, then, was the level of sex-role consciousness arrived at by
Pine Hill boys by the end of third grade. Their picture of themselves
and of their world, of their powers and their options, reflected accu-
rately the models the second curriculum, in both its latent and mani-

fest forms, was presenting to them. The date, it should be remembered, was 1973.

Career Choices of Girls

Even before they had entered first grade the girls had learned to make appropriate career choices for their sex. A three-year-old girl who insisted that the only gift she wanted for Christmas was a doctor's kit because she intended to be a doctor when she grew up, changed her mind at age four and said she intended to be a nurse when she grew up because "I'm not going to turn into a man!"

By the age of six the first-grade girls had long since absorbed the lessons of the second curriculum thoroughly enough to know exactly what motherhood—the one career they all seemed headed for—was all about. Thus Anne could say, "Mothers are the House," and her peers understood her perfectly. Although all the cooking, cleaning, sewing, and child care that took place at home was handled by mother, there was no drudgery or unpleasantness in the role as the first-grade girls perceived it. There was love and fun, and they wanted that fun and love for themselves; they wanted to be mothers. In the following stories the word "housewife" is synonymous with mother.

HOUSEWIFE   Mothers clean the house.
            "Time for bed children!" I will say.
            I will feed my children.—By Karen

HOUSEWIFE   Mothers are the House
            I will feed my children
            I will look in a cook book.—By Anne

HOUSEWIFE   I want to be a housewife.
            I will try my fire.
            I will help my children.—By Mary

HOUSEWIFE   What can a housewife do?
            A housewife can clean the house.
            A housewife cooks the food.—By Andrea

There were a few first-grade girls who wrote about other career choices, but comments made by the girls throughout the school year showed that such choices did not preclude motherhood. In each of these stories the helping component is present. As in the case of the first-grade boys, these choices—nurse and teacher—reflected the careers they had learned about in their social studies unit on Home and Community Helpers.

TEACHER   I want to be a teacher.
           I want to help the children.
           I want to help children learn to read and write.—By Sally

TEACHER   I want to be a teacher.
           Our teacher helps us read in *A Duck Is a Duck*.[8]—By Phyllis

TEACHER   I want to be a teacher.
           I will help children read in *May I Come In?*[9]—By Sarah

NURSE   I want to be a nurse
         Sometimes a nurse,
         Gets to take care of movie stars.—By Tammy

NURSE   I want to be a nurse.
         I want to help sick people.
         I can get the doctor.
         "Nurse, help me get better.
         I want to get better."—By Susan

NURSE   I want to be a nurse.
         A nurse helps the doctor.
         A doctor gives medicine to people.
         A nurse helps the doctor.—By Jennifer

Jennifer and Susan clearly knew that nursing was a job reserved for girls and that the nurse's primary function was to "help" the male doctor. By the age of five they already knew that the important work was reserved for boys and that the supportive function—the back-up work that men chose not to do—was assigned to them.

Bombarded on all sides by the second curriculum, the second-grade girls saw no reason to question the career choices they had made in first grade. They had played the House game (described in chapter 8) and enjoyed the hugging and kissing that had been an important part of that game. So it was not surprising that in response to the question "What do you want to be when you grow up?" the second-grade girls said, "A mother and housewife because it is fun." They saw it as a game; something you play at.

"I just want to stay home and take care of my kids. It is fun," said Terese. "I want to be a mother. It is fun," said Melissa. "I want to be a housewife because I would have fun," said Lori. Jackie wanted to be a mother but she couldn't imagine why. Perhaps she was slow on the uptake or perhaps she thought she didn't need a reason, for all she said was, "A mother because . . ." Carrie said she wanted to be a teacher because this, too, was fun. The insistence on the fun aspects of the roles of mother and teacher was one more example of how far from reality, how wide of the mark, the information they were getting from the second curriculum really was. Recognition of this fact was not to come until later.

The other girls continued to hold on to the first-grade ideal of helping others by serving as a teacher or nurse. Thus Dora said she wanted to be a "nurse because I want to help people," and Sandra said, "A teacher. I will help the children."

Socialized in early childhood and throughout their years in the primary grades to think of themselves as future wives and mothers, the third-grade girls had never thought beyond the sex-role choices presented to them by the second curriculum, especially motherhood. They did not know—and the second curriculum certainly did not teach them—that they would probably spend more of their adult lives working outside the home than in rearing children. The helping motif remained in their ambitions. A bit of adventure and dominance now showed up also. But the big thing in their lives was motherhood, and even though they were nine years old, they could agree with Sally in the "Peanuts" cartoon, who said, at the age of five, "I never said I wanted to be someone. All I want to do when I grow up is be a good wife and mother." The big word in their future was not *money*, as it was coming to be with some of the boys, but *fun*. Thus, barely beyond infancy herself, Angela could say she wanted to have a baby because "it is fun."

Other third graders wrote: "I want to be a plain old woman wife. It is fun" (Megan); "A mother. I want to have a baby. It is fun" (Regina); "I want to be a housewife because it is fun" (Melanie); "I want to be a nurse so I can help people when they are sick" (Elizabeth); "I want to be a nurse. I want to help people when they are sick" (Sonya); "I want to be a nurse. It is a good thing to be" (Elaine); "I want to be a teacher. I just like it" (Laura); "I want to be a teacher to boss the kids around" (Maureen); "I want to be a pet keeper. I would take care of animals" (Monica); "I want to be a storekeeper with lots of candy. I would eat the candy" (Tracey); "I want to be a stewardess. I like to travel" (Donna).

When I first read the career choices of the third-grade girls I thought some progress had been made; at least three girls had chosen pet keeper, candy-shop owner, and stewardess. Then I found the Little Golden Books that told girls and boys what they could be when they grew up, and there were the candy shop owner and the stewardess. The second curriculum had added them to the girls' repertoire.

The powerful impact of the second curriculum was thus clearly demonstrated in the children's responses to questions about career choices. From first through third grade, the boys had broadened their career choices; the girls had restricted theirs to the limited repertoire offered by the second curriculum.

The second curriculum had strong backup. The children themselves were its best supporters, as evidenced by the case of Terri. When Terri entered first grade the teacher did not know whether she was a boy or a girl. Her name was gender-free and she dressed in jeans and a shirt. She had straight black hair that hung to her shoulders, but that provided no clue. The teacher from across the hall suggested that they look at his/her feet. They were short and wide. No clue there either. It was not until Terri lined up with the girls to go to the lavatory that the teacher knew she was a girl. Terri, who was at the head of the class academically and was exceptionally talented in art, was the perfect candidate for the nickname "Tomboy." She had built a fort in the woods, which she shared with the boys, and when the children wrote about careers, Terri wrote:

FOOTBALL PLAYER   I want to be a football player
                   Some of the time one of the players
                   Has to kick the ball.—By Terri

When Terri's story was read to the class, the children laughed. They knew she had failed the second curriculum, and even though the teacher said, "Things are changing, boys and girls, and some day girls will be playing football along with boys, and then you won't laugh," the laughter continued. To emphasize the humor of the idea the boys rolled over on the floor and slapped one another on the back. They made their point.

Quite in contrast was their response to Michael. They listened attentively when his story was read and respectfully refrained from laughing when bumbling Michael made the outrageous claim that he was already a "foxy" football player:

> I am a football player.
> I am in a football game.
> I can get a touchdown, too.
> I can play foxy football.

There was no way that Michael could play even non-foxy football. But his fantasy was not, as in Terri's case, considered untenable.

So much, then, for the role models presented—or, more precisely, hammered in—by the second curriculum. The concepts were failure-proof. There was never any chance that they would confuse the children. With no competing ideas to challenge them, they shaped the mental life of the children so profoundly that it was almost impossible for them to see the reality around them. Although more than four-fifths of the mothers of Pine Hill children were in the labor force, for example, this fact never shook the woman's-place-is-in-the-home image they found in the visual and verbal models that surrounded them. Unlike the children in the Hans Christian Andersen story, these children *could* see the Emperor's clothes. How could they help it? If all the adults in their world saw the raiment, who were mere children to challenge them?

·6·

WHAT WAS BEING LEARNED:
THE BOYS

The school knew a great deal about the academic curriculum and how to scale it to the children's level of development. This curriculum was designed to match the abilities and capacities of the children year by year, grade by grade. The school was well equipped to measure and judge "reading readiness." It knew that the first-grade boys were well prepared for the demands to be made on them. They had the requisites for success. Otherwise they would not have been there. Mountains of research supported the school on this matter. On the side of the children, the academic curriculum, especially reading, had prestige; they all wanted to learn. So did their teachers want them to. The children received lots of help from them.

The second, or sex-role, curriculum was different. It was overwhelming. Living up to the specifications for the male model required extraordinary powers, including the ability to perform deeds that were not all that feasible for boys of barely six. A poem entitled "Boys," which was offered for sale in poster form by the local newspaper, reminded parents and boys what was expected of them. Not just the usual things like being sturdy, strong, courageous, and full of spirit and fun, which they could be; not just exploring, romping, and running, which they could do. That was just the beginning. God wanted more:

> God made the world out of his dreams
> Of magic mountains, oceans, and streams,
> Prairies, and plains, and wooded land.
> Then paused and thought, "I need someone to stand
> On top of the mountains, to conquer the seas,
> Explore the land and climb the trees . . .
> When he had completed the task he'd begun
> He surely said, "That's a job well done."

These were the things expected of men.

The Pine Hill boys knew they were expected to be men, and they saw themselves that way. When they were called boys, they protested, "We're not boys, we're men!" Still there was not one Pine Hill boy—in either the first or the sixth grade—who could have measured up to the specifications God had dreamed up. Not one could have stood on the mountaintops or conquered the seas or tamed the wilderness. It was like asking them to read the *New York Times* before they had mastered their letters. Until they were at least ten years old, in fact, they were not even permitted to go alone into the woods near the school, much less explore the prairies and plains. Literal-minded six-year-old boys could not "pass" these tests as they could, for example, those in reading; that is, on the basis of these standards, they could not prove themselves men. Even on a more mundane level Pine Hill boys fell short. They could not earn a paycheck as their fathers did. They were not invincible. They were merely boys. They may have entered the world as "Daddy's little men," but now they had to validate that claim. They had to become "instant men." Academic requirements were easy by comparison.

Being "Daddy's little man" at home, with all the security and comfort the word "little" evoked, and proving one's manhood in competition with twenty other "instant men" were not at all the same thing. As first-graders, they had entered the real world. Now each boy had to prove himself with his peers and on their own turf, which they themselves would control. In view of their as yet limited talents and abilities, the problem was not a small one. Their solution, as we saw in chapter 2, was to develop their own model for machismo—their own definition of the male role—within the general guidelines set by the adult world, a model on their own scale with standards that were practicable for them. In short, a model they could live up to. Even so, the standards were demanding, as the failure of the "losers" showed.

To arrive at their definition of the male role, the boys drew upon images they had already absorbed from the world around them or had had drummed into them by adults. The boys' formulation of their model took on two aspects, a positive one and a negative one, from which arose a set of prescriptions and proscriptions, Do's and Don'ts. They had already been applying the rules of machismo in setting standards for membership in the Tent Club. By the fourth grade, the male canon was absolutely clear.

The Positive Canon

First, of course, to be a man you had to be willing to fight, whatever the odds. If a boy did not like to fight, it was important to act as though he did, as third-grader Jonathan taught Kenny (chapter 3). As a corollary, being able to take it, to "hang in there," was important, especially if documented by scars. A boy had to play ball—or anything else—"rough" so that he might acquire scars to wear as badges of courage. In fact, the cultivation of scars was almost as important among the boys at Pine Hill as among nineteenth-century German university students. Inventing novel ways to defy authority, to fight the establishment and stay out of trouble, was machismo of the highest order. Physical strength was important. Bravery in the face of danger was important, and if danger did not come it was necessary to go out and court it. Competing was important. Winning, being first, was extremely important. Being a man, then, required a combination of qualities not easily come by, but there was not one Pine Hill boy who did not lay claim to all of them. The evidence of such machismo could be acquired only on the playground, where, with teachers out of the way, the boys were literally on their own turf.

Be Strong

The catalogue of manly qualities codified by the Pine Hill boys themselves placed a heavy emphasis on physical strength. This one characteristic of the male role model, along with being first, stood out above all the rest. It was physical strength that had made second-grader Sean first captain in all the games. It was physical strength that had made third-grader Billy the "cock of the walk" before the third-grade boys organized and used group pressure to control him. So firm was the belief that great physical strength was a given for the male model that when first-grader Scott heard the story of Pippi Longstocking,[1] a young girl with extraordinary strength, he protested, "That isn't true. Girls aren't strong. Boys are strong. Girls are smart"—implying that intelligence was far less valuable than strength.

There were even boys at Pine Hill who made career choices based on their unshakable conviction that since they were males they were also strong. Third-grader Nicky was one of the lightweights in a class where girls were as big and as tall as boys. Yet when asked what he wanted to be when he grew up, he said, "a motorcycle cop. You have to be strong to be a motorcycle cop. And you have to be able to take a physical [examination]. You have to be able to pass a test. And you have to be able to take a beating." From the time he had entered first grade, Nicky, although slightly built, had proved himself in all these areas. He had passed the tests of his peers and had been permitted "in."

I commented to Nicky that a "lot of women are becoming police officers nowadays." Several boys listening to our conversation shrugged their shoulders. "Yeah," Nicky sought to enlighten me, "they're policewomen but none of them are allowed to ride on motorcycles. They can't take the speed and the shifting." From the shrugs and Nicky's tone of voice it was apparent that the boys all considered women as weak as men were strong, and thus incapable of the "hard" work done by men. The second curriculum had taught them that. And it was more convincing than the fact that many women actually did ride motorcycles and were able to handle the shifting. If I had pointed this out to Nicky, he would have had to rationalize the situation or change his career choice. I didn't, but I did ask, "Is shifting hard to do?" "I'll say it is. You have to shift by hand with the motorcycles they have now," he told me. "Could you do that?" I asked. "Yeah," he said, with some annoyance that I would even have to ask.

If nothing was handy to compete for or fight about, one had to go out and find something to overcome. One had to court danger. The scars acquired in derring-do were as valuable as the scars of battle. The third-graders Paul and Derek, for example, laid claim to being the Evel Kneivels of Pine Hill, risking life and limb to ride their minibikes dangerously on the hills behind their homes. "There is this big hill in our woods and there is a path on the hill and Derek and I jumped it with our minibikes. Well, one day it started raining and drizzling and it got real slippery. Well, I was burning [going at such a fast speed that the rubber tires began to smoke] and I went over it when I hit—well, I had an accident and I hit a tree. Then I got up, and Derek did it and he went over and I thought he had broken his leg because he slammed his leg into the tree. But then he got up. That was fun. One back tire was off the ground. Man, that was fun." The more dangerous the sport, the greater the fun.

"If you or Derek had broken your leg would you still have thought that you had had fun?" I asked. "Yeah, sure!" Paul said in a voice that reproached me for having asked the question. A broken leg would have been visible to everyone for at least two months. Then Derek took over the story. "There is this field where the ground is soft so I said to myself, 'if I fall off I won't get hurt. I'll be all right.' So I rode around once and I was all right. Then I let Jeffrey ride. Then I said, 'Oh, heck, this isn't any fun.' And there was a jump on the other hill so I jumped and the wheel went like this [demonstrating how the wheel buckled under his body], and man, that was fun."

I asked the boys for their definition of fun in playing games, and it turned out to be action, adventure, playing rough, courting danger, and acquiring scars. "What is so great about playing rough?" I asked. "MORE ACTION, MAN!" declared third-grader Tommy at the top of his lungs. "Do you mean," I asked, "that playing rough is playing the game the way real adult men play it?" "Yes," said third-grader Derek. "It's more action. You don't feel that you can't do it." Playing rough, then, helped boys feel that they were in the battle to win; that they could do it—even if they were hurt in the process.

I suggested to the third-grade boys that being hurt was a painful experience and that a severe injury could put one of them in the hospital. "That," I said, "can't be called fun, can it?" But third-grader Billy contradicted me. The second curriculum was clear-cut and specific on this point. "It's like my grandaddy says, 'if a boy doesn't have a couple of scars he'll never be a man!'" The very mention of the word "scars" triggered in the third-grade boys an impulse to show off their own scars, those badges of courage that validated their manhood. "I've got a scar here and here," they boasted as they bared arms and legs to provide the best possible view of scars both newly acquired and nearly faded from view. "We've all got scars," said third-grader Jonathan of himself and his friends.

Be First

A hard-and-fast rule of the second curriculum was that boys, no matter how young or small, must strive to be first in all things. The boy whose name would "poll the winning vote" had to prove his leadership ability on the playground as preliminary training for throwing his hat into the presidential ring. So important was being first to the second-grade boys at Pine Hill that before they could play any kind of game, leadership had to be established. Who would be first captain? Usually it was not a discussion among peers that gave a second-grade boy his right to that title but his insistence that if he was not declared first captain he would beat up every boy who challenged his claim. Thus, size and strength were important criteria for "firstness" among second-graders. The first captain reserved the right to appoint his second and third in command, but other titles—fourth captain, fifth captain, and so on—were up for grabs, so the ranking went on until every boy had been judged for leadership, decision-making, and status within the group for each new activity or ball game.

When disputes about leadership arose they were easily solved by "pulling rank." Thus, when second-grader Jeff insisted on a point because he was the captain, Sean retorted, "Yeah, but I'm the first captain. I'm higher than you!" Jeff backed down. "Yeah, that's right," he agreed as he dropped his argument. There was little point in challenging a boy who had proven that he could beat up every other boy in the class. But when a boy thought the odds were with him or when he felt he had no other choice, he did fight. The ability to "stay in there" whatever the consequences was part of the positive sex-role model the boys developed for themselves from the second curriculum.

Being chosen by the teacher to be the line leader was a special kind of winning. As one first-grade boy put it, "It's my best thing [being line leader]." In the sense that the line leader was "in charge" of the line of children who followed, the position was analogous to that of a teacher in the children's minds. A line leader determined how slowly or how fast the rest of the children would walk to get to the restroom, the lunch room, the library, or the playground. At Pine Hill teachers rotated the line-leader position so that no one student ever gained control of it.

The position immediately behind the line leader did not confer any special honor on a child, but everyone wanted to be as near to the line leader as possible, since the closer the child was to the front, the closer he/she was to the coveted first place. Unscrupulous boys and girls would use the second-in-line position to sneak past the line leader to gain control of the line. Such an action often led to fighting, which the teacher would punish by banishing both children to the back of the line.

There were two standard techniques used by Pine Hill primary-age children for moving up in line. One was to ask a friend for permission to stand in front of him/her in the line. Such favoritism generated howls of foul play and demands that the teacher punish the offenders: "Teacher, Yvonne gave Cheryl 'frontsies!' Make them go to the end of the line!" Even greater hostility was shown toward the child who "butted," that is, cut into the line without another child's permission. If the teacher did not remove the offender, he/she would be skillfully punched and kicked by other children. Rarely did such punishment from peers persuade a child who had successfully "butted" to go to the end of the line.[2]

Being first in line was important not just spacially but temporally. The child who was first in line was the first to be served in the cafeteria and had a better choice of where he or she would sit at the lunch tables. The boy who got outside first could choose which ball field the boys would use that day simply by being the first to claim the space. The child who got to the restroom first had his choice of the facilities there. The child who entered the library first had his choice of seats, and that usually meant a dash for the child-sized rockers. In the third grade, however, the once well-ordered line gave way to groups of children walking together in the halls as they went from place to place. The teacher was no longer in complete control of the behavior of boys.

One might think that for boys, the fight to be first would end with written desk work. Not so. Even in this academic task the second-grade boys fought for preeminence in the group. The work did not have to be correctly done, but the page did have to have answers in all the blank spaces. The boy who raced to the bottom of the page first, notified his peers by calling out, "I'm first!" Other voices would quickly claim the rest of the high-status positions. If the teacher subsequently ruled that the papers were incorrect and had to be done again, her orders would most likely be ignored by the winning boys. A failing grade was preferable to loss of rank, and thus status, within the group. Speed could be judged by peers; the teacher could judge only quality.

Not until much later in the school year did the second-grade boys come to place greater value on the quality of their work than on the speed with which it was accomplished. Unsubstantiated claims to first place were no longer acceptable. They had to be proven. Now the boys asked, "Who got the highest grade?" or "Who got the most right?" and only when that had been decided could a boy say, "I'm first!" By the third year the grade, that is, genuine achievement, had become the most important criterion for claiming top status in the academic arena.

In view of the pain and hardship involved in winning male accolades, I asked if it was really worth the effort. It was. For, although the boys might have had occasional moments of self-doubt about their ability to measure up to the male role model, they had no doubt at all about the importance of being a man. They told me how important it was when I asked, "Is it so important to be a man?" "Is it IMPORTANT to be a man? It's VERY IMPORTANT!" The boys saw no reason to explain why. The reason was self-evident. So when I asked, "Why is it so important to be a man?" Chad decided to be kind to me. "Well," he said, "if you're not tough someone will come up to you and start hitting you and you will start bawling your head off. That's what girls do. And everyone will call you sissy and all that stuff. You got to be a little tough. Not like some of these girls." "Then being a man is being tough and not a sissy like the girls?" I asked. "Yeah," they said. That was it. The stereotypes helped the boys maintain the illusion of being real men even though they were only nine years old.

The Negative Canon

The negative aspect of the male canon was totally different. Its demands were in many ways even harder to live up to than the positive ones. The first and most fundamental premise on which the whole male model rested was that machismo was *nonfemale*. Only when this negative criterion had been fulfilled could one claim to have achieved machismo. From this primary and basic component of the sex-role pattern that the boys were piecing together for themselves, there evolved a whole repertoire of taboos. No weakness, no playing with girls, no participation in female activities such as cleaning the classroom, no display of affection. Whatever females did, that was what the boys must *not* do. A boy had to overcome and root out anything in his own actions, feelings, and preferences that could be viewed as even remotely female.

Not only did the boys stake their claim on not *being* a girl or *doing* anything girls did; they went a step further: even associating with girls was not manly. Girls were "sissies," and no self-respecting boy would play with a sissy lest he himself be considered a sissy by his peers. Babies were thought to be a part of the female world, so boys dissociated themselves from babies also. Crying was something both girls and babies did. Being a cry-baby was, therefore, doubly stigmatized. No epithet was more withering. It was to be avoided at any cost. I once heard a nun, the principal of a parochial school, admonish a six-year-old boy who had been hurt on the playground: "Stop crying and behave like a man!" He stopped at once. No order could have been more effective. Or, perhaps, more costly.

Don't Associate with a Sissy

A boy who played with girls was by definition a sissy. Macho boys avoided contact with such boys as much as they shunned girls and the female world. But in the first grade at Pine Hill there was a boy who was so autonomous an individual that he played with Anne, the classmate he liked best, even though she was a girl. Except for his close attachment to Anne, Adam was a loner. He was "out" of the peer group by choice and not because of rejection. He did not want to run with the pack; group membership played no part in his development, cognitively or socially. Although he was at the top of his class in reading, writing, and arithmetic, he was not in the macho race. Through all of the first grade, though not beyond, his autonomy protected him to some extent from the criticism leveled at him by both peers and adults. His attempt to function without regard to the second curriculum ended in second grade when peer pressures—he was called "sissy"—forced him to conform.

Don't Play with a Cry-Baby

When the doors of the school opened in September, Martin's mother was there to see him safely to his classroom, but when she attempted to leave him with the teacher, he cried and clung to her skirts until it was decided that he should go home and return the following day with a friend. None of this escaped his peers.

By November it was evident that Martin lagged behind his classmates in learning to read, although subsequent testing by a psychologist showed that he had above-average intelligence. "I don't know what has happened to Martin," his teacher said. "He was doing so well and now he won't do a thing I ask him to do. What have I done wrong?" A short time later she noted, "Danny doesn't want to play with Martin anymore. Now Danny wants to play with Ryan all the time. The children will play with Martin when I ask them to, but when I don't ask them to, they don't."

No longer interested in learning to read, Martin attempted to enlist the support of the teacher in gaining acceptance by peers. He cried frequently and complained loudly, "No one likes me. No one will play with me. Everyone thinks I'm dumb." On one occasion Ryan responded to Martin's accusations by saying, "He's just saying that because he's bad sometimes. When Ms. Carter is trying to teach us something and we want to hear, then he's bad. So we tell him, 'Shut up so we can hear!'" Ryan had presented a reasonable explanation for not asking Martin to play in an effort to forestall teacher pressures on him to accept this unmanly boy as a playmate. Neither Ryan nor his friends dared risk their own nebulous position in the macho world by playing with a cry-baby. "Go away," peers told him. "You're a cry-baby. You belong in kindergarten." Martin might have been "Daddy's little man" at home, but at school he failed the early tests for manhood.

Don't Do Housework

As the boys in the first and second grades further distanced themselves from the female world, they rejected even classroom activities that they considered inappropriate for boys. It was their good fortune to have female classmates who opted to clean up the classroom, releasing them to go outside and play. And although a teacher might ask a boy to pick up a paper he had thrown on the floor or to clean up his own art space after painting a picture, the major classroom housekeeping tasks—washing blackboards and sinks, for example—fell to the girls.

The boys declared independence from housework vocally as well as in their behavior. On one occasion, for example, the first-grade boys made it known that they would never cook or sew or do any other housekeeping chore under any circumstances, even if they starved to death or had to throw away their torn clothing or go without clothes. First-grader Kevin had responded to the story of Pippi Longstocking by stating emphatically and derisively, "Girls sew!" This was meant as a put-down and was met with peals of laughter from other boys. Making fun of girls was a device used extensively by Pine Hill boys of all ages to distance themselves from girls and to demonstrate their solidarity against the female world. I followed up on Kevin's remark by asking, "What would you do if, when you are grown up, you rip your only shirt and there is no one to sew it for you? Wouldn't you sew it then?" Kevin's answer was an emphatic "No!" As our conversation ended, additional peer laughter rewarded Kevin for his macho stand against sewing and confirmed the correctness of his solution. "We wouldn't sew. That's girl stuff," they said. They had made it clear that they held not only sewing but the girls who did the sewing in low esteem.

In the second grade the boys' resistance to housework went beyond refusal to clean the classroom with the girls to refusal to become involved in housekeeping chores even symbolically. The teacher had used the old familiar song "This is the way we go to school" to teach the children the days of the week. The girls lustily sang their way through a week of activities that included washing clothes, ironing, sewing, cleaning, baking, and marketing, while the boys sat stodgily in their seats. Only when the song came to Sunday did they show that they were aware of the lesson being taught: then they rested ostentatiously with arms and legs sprawling over their desks.

When the lesson was over, I asked the boys, "What would you do if you lived alone and there was no one to cook for you? Would you cook for yourselves?" "No way!" In their answers they were as positive as the first-grade boys had been when they had said that they preferred nakedness to sewing a rip in their best shirts. "I'll starve to death before I'll cook," proclaimed Sean, thereby putting his masculine pride ahead of his life. And it was not only Sean who would have sacrificed life and limb before he would have admitted to being less than the most macho of men. "I'm never going to do any of those things," said Barry. "That's for girls!" The boys now began to vie among themselves to show their contempt for housework. "How do you plan to keep your house clean and have food to eat?" I asked. It was Sean who answered, for all the boys, "I'll get a wife for that!"

Although in their rejection of housework the boys were obeying one of the commandments implicit in the second curriculum— "Thou shalt not be responsible for housework"[3]—more was involved. Rejection of housework itself was not new; that had begun in first grade. What was new was getting a wife to do the housework they did not want to do themselves. They considered it their birthright to decide not only how they should spend their own time and energies but also how their future wives should. They were, in effect, expressing what the second curriculum had taught them—to look on marriage not as a shared relationship but as one in which a man "got a wife" to do the work he did not want to do. They were already voicing their supposed authority over the destines of the little girls who might one day become their wives.

Don't Show Affection

If neither foes nor loving friends can hurt you,
    If all men count with you, but none too much!
Yours is the Earth and everything that's in it.
    And—which is more—you'll be a man, my son.[4]

The second curriculum showed no quarter to the boy who—like a girl—demonstrated emotion or a need for affection. Emotion and affection would interfere with their male destiny. Men were "Jack-the-Giant-Killers." They were the problem-solvers, the sleuths, the pioneers, the adventurers, and the explorers. Dependence on affection would make them vulnerable to those who would prey on their weakness. This Kiplingesque denial of emotional needs was, in my opinion, one of the cruelest demands of the male role-model of the second curriculum.

It was not until second grade that the second-curriculum rules governing emotion and affection were thoroughly integrated into the male sex-role model the boys were developing for themselves. We recall that before they began to feel compelled to assume the "cool," "tough guy" image greatly admired by second-graders and older children, the kindergarten and first-grade boys had sat comfortably on their teachers' laps and basked in the affection bestowed on them. When one of the first-grade teachers had had to take long-term leave, the boys as well as the girls had missed the loving support they had become accustomed to, and a few were totally devastated by her absence. Jimmy, for example, became a problem in the classroom and on one occasion had to be sent to the office to be disciplined. The principal, searching for the cause, took Jimmy on his lap and asked, "Do you miss Ms. Minor?" Tears welled up in Jimmy's eyes. "Is it the hugs she always gives you?" he asked. Jimmy nodded his head. "I miss her, too," the principal replied, "but while she is gone you will have to try to be very good for Ms. Taylor and whenever you think you need a hug, just come to the office and I'll find one for you. You can also go to see Ms. Best. She has lots of hugs for children." With such reassurance, Jimmy was able to promise that he would be "good" for the substitute teacher. First-grade boys had also sought affection from one another, as when they tumbled over other boys on the floor and the playground. They could even hug and kiss the girls in the class when they role-played the father or child in the House game (described in chapter 8).

Even at the beginning of the second grade, boys had been able to show affection to peers. But as the year progressed and the second-curriculum rules for the male sex role began to jell, the second-grade boys learned to limit or disguise their physical contact. Fighting, for example, was a good way to have physical contact in an approved fashion. An arm thrown casually around another boy's shoulder as they walked on the playground was another acceptable way. So, also, was falling into one another's arms in fits of laughter over a joke, preferably at the girls' expense, for this permitted affectionate contact along with male solidarity vis-à-vis outsiders.

If this "be a nonfemale" lesson was cruel, so was the teaching of it. It was not unusual for Pine Hill mothers to report that their sons had arrived home in tears because peers had called them "fags," "queers," or "gay." Pine Hill's second-grade boys might not have understood the precise definition of any of these terms, but they did know that they referred to a weakness in a boy's emotional armor. Even verbal affirmation of emotional support was denied the boys by their evolving version of the second curriculum, as Phillip learned on one occasion. He had lost his free play time one morning because he had not finished his desk work, and his feeling of self-worth was badly in need of restoration. He looked around and approached James. "James is my best friend," he said, "so I'm putting my pencil down here beside him. You *are* my best friend, aren't you, James?" Every child in the class heard Phillip's bid for emotional support from James. Phillip waited. The class waited. The reassuring words never came. James maintained a steady gaze at the paper on his desk as he pretended to be oblivious to the boy standing anxiously beside him. "You *are* my best friend, aren't you, James?" Phillip repeated frantically. In the long silence that followed, Phillip knew he had lost. James would never say publicly that they were friends. "Your name is Pope 'cause it rhymes with dope!" Phillip said angrily. He picked up his pencil and went back to his desk. But the children, both boys and girls, knew that it was Phillip and not James who was the "dope." Phillip had shown that he was emotionally needy, vulnerable. No male model in the second curriculum permitted that.

Rudyard Kipling's "If," cited above, advised young men of yet another, and perhaps more dangerous, emotional hazard to be avoided: that of caring more for a friend than for oneself. It was a lesson learned early by Pine Hill boys, who did not seek one or two best friends, as was the custom with girls, but, rather, bonded in groups of pals, buddies, and teammates. Having a peer group not only facilitated the games boys played but protected them from the emotional investment girls made in best friends, thereby insuring that no boy would feel compelled to sacrifice his place in the winner's circle for a peer. Not one Pine Hill boy could have remotely understood the motivations of Whittier's champion speller who lamented to the boy she loved, "I'm sorry that I spelt the word; I hate to go above you. Because . . . you see, I love you."[5] Such denigration of self was a part of the female world and alien to the male world. Even the biblical ideal of the man who gave up his life to prove his love for his friend was contrary to the model for maleness developed by the Pine Hill boys. Sentiment would not rob them of their place in the sun.

To test just what boys would do to show their devotion to their friends, I presented a hypothetical situation to the third-graders. "Suppose," I began, "that Dennis and Randy, two very good friends, decided to compete against one another for the quarterback position on the football team. Dennis knows that Randy wants to win that position more than he wants anything in the whole world, but Dennis has stronger legs and can run faster than Randy. He also has stronger arms and can throw a ball farther than Randy. And, although Dennis would like to play the quarterback position, it isn't as important to him as it is to Randy. So should he let Randy win the competition?" "No," they told me. "Why not?" I asked. "Randy will be broken-hearted if he doesn't get to play quarterback. Shouldn't Dennis, who is Randy's best friend, let him win the competition?" The boys were of one mind on this issue. "No," they said emphatically. "A man has his pride and he doesn't want to lose it." Derek put it another way. "You have your reputation in the school and you don't want to lose it." I asked the boys, "Is your pride more important than your friend's happiness?" "Sure," they agreed, "you have your pride and you don't want to lose it because then people won't think you're so great." Then Chad showed once more how well he understood the rules of the second curriculum. "Your guys won't like you as much if you lose your pride," he said.

The primary-age boys at Pine Hill understood Kipling perfectly. They had to pledge a certain amount of loyalty to one another, but they had to restrain themselves lest they form too close an attachment to any one friend and thus let affection rob them of their proof of manhood: the blue ribbon or the trophy that bore the legend "First Place."

The Costs of Machismo

So great was the need to be first, to win, and thus to prove themselves real men that the second-grade boys often got in their own way and lost out entirely. The competition and aggression of the male style of relating became counterproductive, as the following two episodes will illustrate. In both these instances, while the boys were fighting the battle, the girls were achieving the goal.

The second-grade class had their collective eye on an incubator in the room that had been filled with twelve eggs now about to hatch. A chart in the front of the room listed carefully worked out plans that the children were to follow when the long-awaited event finally happened in the spring. All contingencies had been taken into consideration so that the children would derive the greatest benefit from this experience. After what seemed to them an endless amount of time, the day finally arrived when the first eggshell broke and the bill of a tiny chick began to peck its way out. Every ear in the class heard that eggshell break, and the children knew exactly what was happening. The girls waited at their desks for instructions on how to proceed. The boys didn't wait for anyone or anything. As a group they jumped to their feet and started toward the incubator shouting, "I'm in charge! I'm in charge!" The boys nearest the incubator were pulled away by other boys shouting, "I'm in charge and you can't watch until I say when!"

The pushing and pulling quickly turned into full-scale fighting. David practiced his karate kick on Sean, who fell to the floor in pain and then got up and delivered an even stronger kick to David. The familiar playground pattern of fighting to determine who would be in charge was working itself out in the classroom. The boys would not listen to the long-term substitute teacher trying to stop the fighting. The noise echoed up and down the halls.

The girls meanwhile did not take part in the fight. They wanted to see the chicks hatch as much as the boys did, but they had no compulsion to be in charge. Now, however, that the careful plans were not being implemented, they had to improvise. One girl climbed onto a table overlooking the incubator and out of range of the fighting, which now occupied the center of the room. Other girls joined her on the table and those for whom there was no room stood on chairs that they pushed into the same area. Their strategy worked, for from their vantage point they could ignore the boys and, totally absorbed, watch the whole process as the chicks hatched. This was, after all, the "moment of truth" for which the entire class had been waiting ever since the incubator had been introduced into the classroom. This was the miracle they had been so long anticipating. The girls saw it all. By the time the boys had fought out the precedence problem, the show was over.

The boys sometimes lost out on the fun of the classroom as well as the learning experiences. On one occasion the teacher told the second-grade boys and girls that they would have the opportunity to make their own kites to fly in the all-school kite-flying contest. Awards were to be given to the child who flew his/hers the highest, had the most original design, or kept his/her kite in the air for the longest period of time. This event was one of the most exciting of the school year.

When the project began the classroom was unusually quiet, for the children were totally absorbed with their own ideas and materials. Then two paper "parachutes" (a variation on the paper airplane) flew through the air. With so much construction paper available to them, two boys had decided to use some of it to see which one could make the parachute that would stay longest in the air. Their peers saw the flying parachutes and decided that this challenge had to be met. Apparently, once the gauntlet had been thrown down—once the first parachute had flown through the air followed by a competing parachute—the rest of the boys had no choice but to rise to the occasion. Within seconds every boy in the room had abandoned the kite-making project to launch parachutes. Having begun the parachute competition, the boys could not stop until they had determined who was first in parachute flying. Claims of being first came from so many boys that they had to resort to fighting to decide just who could claim that honor.

The principal of the school heard the sounds of fighting and rushed to the second-grade classroom. He sent all of the boys home for the rest of the day. As a result, the boys had no kites to fly on the day of the contest. They expressed great bitterness at losing out on all the fun. The girls, who had not been distracted by the parachute competition, finished their kites and won all the prizes.

Outsiders: Cases in Point

When boys as a group lost out on learning experiences or the fun of flying kites, they did not also lose macho points with peers since they were all in the same boat. But when individual boys seeking to prove their machismo violated the rules of the second curriculum so that their action embarrassed peers, they were punished. They were rejected. Other boys would not play with them.

It was not altogether clear why some boys found it difficult, if not impossible, to break the code of the boys' version of the second

curriculum. The peer group lived in a world of common expecta-
tions, but not all the boys were able to read the signs and signals
being beamed out to be them by parents, teachers, the media, and
peers. Howard S. Becker reminds us of the importance of being able
to do so:

> All social groups make rules and attempt, at some time and under
> some circumstances, to enforce them. Social rules define situations
> and the kinds of behavior appropriate to them, specifying some ac-
> tions as "right" and forbidding others as "wrong." When a rule is
> enforced, the person who is supposed to have broken it may be seen
> as a special kind of person, one who cannot be trusted to live by the
> rules agreed upon by the group. He is regarded as an outsider.[6]

At Pine Hill one sign that a boy understood the code of machismo
was his ability to "play it cool," to be "hard" or "tough." A boy who
was cool, hard, or tough did not have to crow about it; his machismo
was self-evident. Being a braggart was, therefore, a sign of weakness.
Being the "boss" was machismo of a high order, but pretending to be
in charge of others without the necessary clout to enforce one's position was not. Boys guilty of such pretense suffered the same fate as
those boys whose behavior had been labeled "female."

Boys commonly asserted a vicarious male identity, by way of their
fathers—the "my father is bigger than your father" or "my father can
lick your father" ploy. In the case of first-grader Scott, the claims
involved the additional macho element of guns. It all began when
Scott passed Danny, a classmate, in the hall and tripped him so that
his face hit the floor and his lip was bruised. "Why did you hit
Danny?" the teacher asked when Scott returned to the classroom.
Scott glanced around the room and saw that every eye was on him,
so with a casual air of bravado and defiance meant to impress his
peers he answered, "Because I wanted to. I just felt like tripping him
so I did." Scott's unspoken question, "So what do you think you can
do about it?" was clearly expressed by his tone of voice and his
unflinching eye-to-eye contact with the—substitute—teacher. She
took up the challenge. "Well, I feel like tripping you and making you
fall on your face, so should I?" she asked. Taken aback by this remark, Scott countered with a threat, "I'll get my father to bring his
gun up here and shoot you." Before the teacher could answer, Danny
shouted, "My father has a gun, too."

The competition between Scott and Danny piqued the interest of
the other boys in the class, and they joined the conversation. "My
father has three guns," one boy said. Then, for the first time in a
classroom situation, they all entered into a competitive game that
was to last for several years, all vying, in this instance, for the pres-

tige that went with gun-owning fathers. With such support thrown to his side, Danny grew braver and openly threatened Scott, "I'm going to have my father bring his gun to school and shoot you!"

Now that Scott was surrounded by boys all testifying to the fact that their fathers also had guns, his bravado wilted. His bluff had been called. He backtracked. "I don't think my father has a gun anymore. Anyway, I didn't say my father has a gun. He doesn't have a gun!" There was no place in the world of six-year-old boys for such a child. He had been forced to backtrack, to retreat. His peers shunned him.

The faux pas of pretending to be someone important, someone older who had power over others, when clearly you were not, was referred to by first-graders and older children as "acting big." Accusations of this nonmacho behavior were leveled at Douglas, who often raged at other children as a storm trooper might to his underlings. He sought to establish his mastery of his version of the second curriculum through intimidation and blustering commands. On one occasion when the children were playing games in the classroom, Douglas "acted big." Standing at his desk, he asked in a loud and accusing voice, "Well, who put this in my school box? Speak up! Who did it? I want a correct answer. Tell me if someone told you to do it!" Every eye in the room was drawn to the piece of metal Douglas was holding in his hand. Jeff said, "It must have been Danny. He's laughing his head off." For a brief moment Douglas looked at Danny, a popular, high-status boy, and then turned his attention to Jeff. "Come here to me, Jeff, I have some questions for you to answer," he said in the same authoritative tone of voice. But Jeff had seen Douglas's fear of challenging Danny and, ignoring the bravado, turned his back on Douglas and resumed his game.

Douglas's attempt to "rule the roost" through verbal force rather than by competing with peers as an equal backfired. He had just shown his classmates that he was "all mouth and no action." When he had the opportunity to prove himself a winner—as in the confrontation with Danny—he had backed down. Even the girls told him he was just "acting big."

These, then, were the criteria of the male role that the boys arrived at on the basis of what they were supplied by adults, media, and their own experience. The enforcement of the proscriptions and prescriptions was largely in their own hands, and they were capable of treating one another far more harshly than the adults treated them.

·7·

WHAT WAS BEING LEARNED:
THE GIRLS

In most studies of elementary-school children, the girls have been relatively neglected. And many mea culpas are called for here, for I too gave the girls in the primary grades short shrift in the first year of my study. This, I now admit, was itself a form of sexism. The original purpose of the study was to test the hypothesis that for boys membership or nonmembership in the peer group affected reading achievement; since girls did learn to read, there seemed little point in spending a lot of time studying their social structure. So I said when I was asked what the girls were saying and doing. It was not that they were worth less research attention, I said, but that the sex-role socialization process going on among boys was more dramatic. More was happening in the boys' world. The little girls were exactly like little girls. That is, they read well, they were nurturant and helpful, they had stronger ties to their teachers, they role-played Mother in the House game, and they chased boys on the playground and kissed them. Nothing new there. Their role called for continuity with the female world of the classroom rather than, as with the boys, a break from it. The girls could amble leisurely, at their own pace, in the direction of womanhood, while the boys had to be instant men the moment they became first-graders. Since boys had to pay their dues in the male club early—while girls began to pay the costs of the female role only later—I clearly needed to concentrate on the boys' world. Observation of the girls' world could wait.

I was wrong. Under the deceptively simple surface, interesting processes were at work among the girls as well as among the boys. But the ambience was quite different. After the almost painful picture of the boys' world and its impact on the rejected boys, entering the girls' world was like moving from a dark and fearful forest into a sunny valley. Here there was nothing that led to stealing, to the killing of animals, to the throwing of stones at adults, or to threats to sue or shoot teachers. There was much that led to rewards.

The girls came to school already primed for the archetypical feminine role. They could exchange affectionate hugs with one another or with the teacher without generating negative comment, while boys had to create a situation of mutual "kidding" or "play fighting" to gain access to physical contact with peers. The girls offered help to teachers and classmates—especially male class-mates—and, as we saw in chapter 5, it was not just "pretend help." In this helpful behavior, Pine Hill girls resembled little girls from many cultures. Maccoby and Jacklin, for example, report the findings of Whiting and Pope in six cultures around the world to the effect that "during the ages of 7 to 11 . . . girls emerge strongly as the more helpful sex."[1] Even before the age of seven—in fact, as early as the age of six—Pine Hill's little girls were already helping.

There were usually little girls busily scrambling around the class-room to provide assistance whenever needed. And there were often little boys sitting passively by, waiting for someone to help them. Thus, for example, during the first-grade testing period, each child had been given a seven-page booklet with instructions to open it, find the correct page, and then fold the booklet back so that only the page on which they were to work would be face up on their desks. Some of the children did this quickly and easily; others could not manage without help. In both first-grade classrooms, little girls who had completed the task looked around the room to see what other children were doing. When they saw classmates having difficulty they got up from their seats and, without a word, did the task for them and sat down. The same helpful acts were repeated as the children progressed through the booklet.

Except for three girls who needed such help, all the helped chil-dren had been boys, and all the helping children, girls. None of the boys had offered help to another child, boy or girl. No one thanked the helping girls. Helping behavior was already expected from them.

Closely related to such helping behavior, but on a less personal level, was a kind of behavior that Maccoby and Jacklin, citing Whit-ing and Pope, described as being "accompanied by a form of domi-nance called 'suggesting responsibility.' "[2] This category included instances in which a child would attempt to control another child in the interests of that other child's well-being or safety. Helping could thus sometimes be a positive aggressive activity. Maccoby and Jack-lin give as illustrations: "Warning a child not to go near a dangerous cliff or insisting that the child come in to a meal."[3] First-grader Krista demonstrated this kind of helping behavior the day she saw a boy's legs dangling from an upstairs window in the school and knew that it would take only one push from a joking friend to send the boy sprawling onto the sidewalk. Disobeying the school rules, she ran quickly to her classroom and told her teacher, "Get Alan out of the window in Ms. Andrew's room. He'll get hurt." Krista gained nothing from this "controlling" act. She did not even think of it in such terms.

Similarly, second-grader Vicki became concerned about Sean, who was risking life and limb to demonstrate to his peers his bravery and skill on the monkey bars. A mishap might well have resulted in serious injury. Children had been known to break bones on the monkey bars even when they had played in a safe manner. So Vicki cautioned Sean, "You're acting silly," and added a threat. "If you don't behave I'm going to tell [the teacher]." Probably glad to be rescued from his derring-do, Sean retreated. A more familiar scene was one of girls warning other children who ran in the halls or on the school steps, "Don't run! You'll get hurt!" Helping was, then, often a way of taking charge when another child put himself/herself in danger. In all these examples of nurturing, of comforting, of responsibility-taking, the little girls were not pretending any more than they were in their helpful acts; they were not play-acting but actually performing a nurturant function. In this sense they were already "little women." But in their own way, they were also "little men." That is, they were aggressive, but aggressive with a feminine touch. In fact, much of their helpful behavior could be characterized as a form of pro-social aggressiveness.

Aggression is one of the variables almost always reported as more frequent among boys than among girls. If aggressiveness is characterized by an intent to hurt, the Pine Hill data confirm the greater incidence of aggressiveness among boys than among girls. Not only did the boys seek to hurt others; they even, as we know, sought scars as proof that they had been hurt themselves. If, however, aggressiveness is conceived of simply as a positive, active kind of behavior that does not necessarily imply hurt, the girls at Pine Hill surpassed the boys in it. The incidents with Krista and Vicki described above are examples of situations in which a girl attempted to control— "boss" would be a possible synonym—another child as a way of assuring the well-being of that child rather than as a way to hurt him or as a way to exercise power.

In the first grade, it was not easy to distinguish the dominance the little girls showed when they role-played the mother in the House game or the teacher in the School game from aggressiveness. Not only did the first-grade girls initiate and conduct these games, but they also exerted considerable control over the other players. On one occasion, for example, first-grader Christine taught a spelling lesson to the children who sat at her feet. She patiently went through each word, imitating the way the teacher taught spelling to her. When she thought she had covered the lesson thoroughly enough, she lovingly patted Julie. "Tell Julie you like her." "I like you Julie," the obedient pupils sang. Then Christine hugged all her pupils—a group that included boys as well as girls—and told them how good they had been. She was definitely the "boss" of that game.

In chapter 8, we will see that the mother role also gave girls the opportunity to be in charge, as did chasing, catching, and kissing boys. The effect of all these activities, however, was to give girls the impression that being a mother, a teacher, or a woman sharing physical contact with men conferred power on them; they were in control, they were in charge. They reveled in the feeling of being an important person vis-à-vis others in these role-playing games. The hidden joke was that no one ever told them that adult women in these roles had no power at all—that men would be running the show.

In keeping with the feminine role the girls offered emotional as well as practical support to those who needed it. They were alert to any situation in which a classmate—more often than not a boy—was having trouble, and they knew precisely what kind of intervention would be most helpful. On one occasion when Martin sat at his desk and cried that no one liked him or would play with him, Joey, a boy new to the class, did try to comfort him. But his resources were limited. "They do like you, Martin," was all he could think to say or do. "No, they don't, you know they don't," Martin replied—with one eye on Ryan and his friends to see what kind of response he was getting—and this Joey could not deny. "They think I'm dumb," Martin added. Then, Jeanette, moved by Martin's tears, came to the rescue. Her resources were far more extensive than Joey's. She knew mere denial would not do. More sublety was called for. She approached me. "Martin has a very nice coloring book," she said. "I think he'd show it to you if you'd ask him." I did not even have to ask. Martin brought his coloring book out of his desk and motioned to me to look at his pictures. It so happened that they were, as Jeanette had said, very beautiful. When he came upon a page that had angry circles scribbled over it, he said, "Now who do you suppose did that?" I assured him that this one picture did not make his coloring book less attractive and Jeanette's concurrence eased his embarrassment. The incident left its imprint on him. With peer support forthcoming only from Joey, a boy whose unkempt appearance and strong unwashed body odor had hindered his own acceptance by peers, the support of even a girl was welcomed by Martin. Jeanette felt no need for praise from me. She had intuited what was called for and had done it.

The following summer he attended summer school, and his teacher, wanting to praise him, said, "Martin colors very nicely." I told her I knew all about his artistic ability, that Julie had drawn my attention to it some months before. "That wasn't Julie," Martin corrected me, "that was Jeanette." My notes showed that Martin had correctly remembered who it was who had supplied him with emotional support when male peers could not. Girls knew how; boys, apparently, did not.

On another occasion, when the school had been able to get a copy of the film *J.T.*—an award-winning television play on the CBS "Children's Hour" about a ten-year-old black child who lived in an inner-city slum area—it was not the poverty of the child's life or the overburdened working mother (all too familiar to many of the children, for they, too, were poor) that disturbed them, but the violent death of the boy's cat at the hands of older boys. J.T. had found the old, one-eyed, badly hurt cat in a junk-filled empty lot and had lavished on him all the love he was unable to express to people around him. Although the film ended on a happy note—J.T. got another cat and an after-school job—the trauma in the film left many of the viewers sobbing in grief, for as first-graders they were not yet ashamed to cry. First-grader Meg put her arm around Tony's shoulder and said, "Don't cry. It's only a movie." In similar fashion first-grader Anne attempted to comfort Michael. Even in the third grade there were some boys who still cried and girls who comforted them. What seemed to me to be significant, however, was not that the boys themselves did not offer comfort to others, but that the clear assigning of the nurturant role left the boys free to be receivers, not givers, of emotional support.

There were vast differences in the friendship relations of boys and of girls. The most salient difference was the presence among some boys but not among any of the girls, of "fake-liking," the manipulative, exploitative use of peers for ulterior ends, which, as reported earlier, became evident in the third grade. There was no such manipulative use of affection among girls. The term "fake-like" was not even in their vocabulary. They might promise, bargain, and negotiate—"if you'll like me, I'll like you" or "if you'll be good to me, I'll be good to you"—but, in the primary grades, there was no evidence of the use of friends for ulterior purposes. There were arguments, fights, and disagreements, but there was, nevertheless, room for open and above-board coalitions, as in the case of Debbie and Vicki in the second grade.

Debbie had written a story for creative writing that had brought her lavish praise from her teacher. She proudly bragged about her story to her friends and repeated her teacher's words over and over. Vicki's story had received only a nod of acceptance, so she angrily told Debbie, "you think you're smarter than anyone else and I'm not going to play with you anymore." Vicki then urged other girls in the classroom not to play with Debbie because "She acts so smart all the time." Debbie was crushed. The hurt she felt could be seen in the tears brimming in her eyes. She approached Vicki and said, "I like you and if you'll be good to me then I'll be good to you. OK?" Vicki again reproached Debbie and Debbie once more pleaded with her. Finally Vicki gave in to Debbie's pleading and said, "OK, but don't act so smart anymore." Self-congratulation about achievement was acceptable in the boys' world, but, apparently, not in the girls'.

Options Available to Girls

There was a wider range of options in the girls' world than in the boys'. These options showed up in a number of areas, in play and games, for example, and, most significantly, even in selection of gender.

Play and Games

Despite the fact that the kindergarten teacher firmly believed that the doll house was the exclusive domain of girls and the large and small building equipment and wheeled toys most appropriate for boys, the girls in fact played with the building equipment as frequently as the boys did. I never saw a boy playing in the doll house, however.

In the base year of the study I had seen many girls playing ball games with boys. At first it had seemed to me that the boys did not object and that, in fact, there were some girls who were such exceptionally good ball players that the boys welcomed them on their teams. Four years later, Tracey was to tell a television interviewer that it had not been that simple. The boys had *not* wanted girls playing with them, and only when a girl had gained permission to play or was recruited to play because one of the boys' teams needed an extra player was a girl really given the opportunity to play. However, once a girl had established herself as an expert ball player and an asset to the team, the decision to play or not to play on any given day was made by the girl herself. Not so with the boys. Because of their stringent macho requirements, a boy had to play ball whether he wanted to that day or not, for this was a requirement for acceptance by peers.

Sean very much wanted Julia, a second-grader, to play on his ball team. She was one of the best ball players in the class, but there were many times when she did not want to play with boys, preferring to spend time with her girl friends. Sean found her independence annoying. She told him on one occasion, "No, I'm not going to play with you today. I'm going to play with Candy." Angered by her refusal—no boy would have dared reject Sean—he threatened, "If you don't play on my team, I'm going to beat you up." Julia was not intimidated. "If you try to beat me up, I'll beat you up. I'm not going to play ball today." And she didn't. A boy could not have made such a personal choice. Julia had more freedom. She played when that was what she wanted to do; if not, she could refuse. And she was willing to fight for the privilege of making her own decisions. She lost nothing by her decision to play ball with the boys. She did not need to acquire scars to wear as badges of honor, although she did need to prove her skill on the ball field to the boys.

For Sean, however, the story was quite different. He was the team captain. His glory depended on having the winning team. He needed her more than she needed him, at least on the ball field. Away from the ball field, it is interesting to note, Julia was not an asset to Sean; she was not invited to his birthday party, an exclusively male event. Julia had no relevant chips in that game.

Fighting

Boys had to fight when challenged if they were to be regarded by other boys as real men, but a girl could opt not to fight if she preferred not to, and no one would call her a "sissy." Most of the girls did fight. They fought with their fists just as the boys fought. But, unlike the boys, they did not usually initiate the fighting. They fought when they felt they had to defend themselves from something the boys had said or done, or they fought in defense of a friend. The highest compliment any Pine Hill boy could make about a girl was to say, "she fights as good as any boy"—to which he always added, "except me."

Monica was one girl who did not like fighting—she was, in fact, fearful of fighting—and she could get out of a fight without humiliation. She had, for example, sat across the lunch table from Denver one day when his attention had been drawn toward his friends in the second grade. While he was engaged in conversation with them, Monica took and ate his potato chips. When he found them missing he howled, "OK who took my potato chips?" No one answered, but he knew instinctively that it had been Monica. He threatened, "I'm going to beat you up when we get outside today, Monica. You took my potato chips." Monica did not answer, but Brenda asked, "What are you going to do?" "I'm going to beat her up," Denver repeated. Brenda then told Monica, who so far had not spoken one word, that she would fight with her. She recruited Elizabeth, Laura, and Donna to strengthen their forces. "If you're going to get that many girls then I'll get Kenny and [second-graders] Sean and Don to fight with me," replied Denver. The organizers of the fight, Brenda and Denver, then agreed that fists would be the only weapons they would use.

When the arrangements had been finalized and it seemed certain there would have to be a fight, Monica turned to me and asked, "Do you want to call off the game?" "What game?" I asked. "Do you mean the fight?" "Yeah, do you want to call it off?" Her insistence cued me in. "That would seem to be a good idea. Someone could get hurt in a fight." My support gave her what she had wanted, an honorable retreat. "OK, Ms. Best wants to call off the game so we're not going to do it," Monica announced in a loud voice. There were no protests. There was no hurling of names such as "sissy." The fight never took place. There was nothing to be gained from fighting a girl who would not fight back.

A girl could get away with such a retreat; a boy, never. For this brief period of time in their lives the girls were free to be either tomboys or little ladies, or both, as they pleased. They had even more. They had the privilege of changing gender identity, of becoming boys. It was a privilege that the boys very definitely did not have.

An Important Option: Gender

Girls into Boys.   The privilege of selecting one's gender was one of the most startling aspects of the girls' androgynous world. The case of Tracey illustrates how it worked. Tracey was a third-grader who preferred ball playing to hopscotch and jump rope. She later indicated that she well understood that boys did not want girls playing with them so she did what she felt she had to do to gain her objective: she changed gender.

Since gender is a social as much as a biological phenomenon, she did not have to worry about changing her body. All that she had to change was the behavior of others—especially of boys—toward her. She had to get their approval of her gender change. She laid the groundwork until she could pass any of the tests they might apply. She could run as fast and play ball as well as any of the boys. She was, in fact, an asset to any team. She fought when fighting was called for. She wore boys' jeans and shirts and walked as much like a boy as possible. So when she was ready she asked the boys if they would let her become a boy. Yes, they said, since she performed so well she could be a boy. Did that mean she could play ball with them? Yes, she could play ball with them. She developed a vocabulary of four-letter words so that she could hold her own in disputes with the boys. She was, it became obvious to all, a boy. The final test came when she asked to belong to the Tent Club. Yes, she could become a member of the club. But never, as it turned out, a full-fledged member. She did not attend meetings or know their secrets. The boys had made an unusual concession—she had, after all, been in their group since kindergarten—to a girl who just happened to be the finest athlete in the class. But of course there had to be limits.

Not every androgynous girl wanted to change her gender identity and be a boy. Regina was almost as good as Tracey on the ball field and more often than not Regina would play on a ball team at free play. The teacher, recognizing Regina's ability on the ball field, made her team captain when they played ball at physical education periods. The boys did not challenge Regina's leadership as they did Benny's when the teacher made him referee of the Greek dodge game. Regina's ability was respected. But that did not mean that the boys agreed that conferring the status of team captain on Regina had been a good idea. Jonathan, in particular, didn't think it was. "I don't like Regina Loghead [a play on her name, Woodstock]. Ms. North lets her be captain of the team and then she sends me out into the field and I never get to bat. Regina Loghead wants to play pitcher and first baseman at the same time," he grumbled. How unreasonable could you get?

Because no team composed of boys wanted too many girls around bothering them, Regina and Tracey always played on opposing teams. They were as competitive as any two boys vying for first place, and the hostility between them often erupted into quarrelling and fighting. On one occasion Regina declared a player on Tracey's team "out" at first base. Tracey did not agree so she shouted, "He was safe, you fat cow!" The verbal argument turned into a physical one. When Tracey's blows became harder and more frequent than her own, Regina ran across the playground toward the school with Tracey in hot pursuit. "When I catch you, you fat cow, I'm going to kill you. He was safe!" Tracey screamed as she narrowed the distance between herself and Regina. Only the intervention of the playground aide stopped the fight.

Regina could have been regarded as a boy if she had wanted to be, for once the gender-change precedent had been established it was available to other girls, too. The following year in the fourth grade, Sonya also took advantage of it. She petitioned to become a boy and permission was granted. Not many girls were interested in changing their gender, however, so although the privilege was there to girls who qualified, Tracey and Sonya were the only two girls who used it. They accomplished this by the simple means of asking the gatekeepers, the boys, and passing the tests. It was no big deal. In the case of boys, however, it was impossible, out of the question. There was no way to change gender and become girls. Boys did not have a gender choice. "Gynandry"[4] was unthinkable.

Boys into Girls.   Although in the adult world more men than women undergo the trauma of transsexual operation, in the world at Pine Hill, male gender-change was impossible even to contemplate, as the case of Ronnie exemplifies. Ronnie had good reason to want to become a girl. Girls had been more successful than he in being accepted by his male peers. Both the androgynous and the traditional girls had some kind of interaction with the boys in the Tent Club, while he had none at all. The androgynous girls played the boys' games with them and the traditional girls chased them across the playground and kissed them. Whichever way it went, the girls in his classroom had more contact with his peers than he had been permitted to have. The androgynous girls had passed all the tests; the traditional girls had not been subjected to any. No wonder, then, that being a girl seemed to Ronnie far better than the situation in which he found himself. It even seemed to him that girls were "smart" and he was not. But gender change in his case was impossible. The children could not imagine such a thing. A boy who wanted to be a girl? It was equivalent to growing three heads.

Denver, Elizabeth, and Laura were the first children to hear Ronnie say, "From now on I'm going to be a girl!" They had stared at him in disbelief. Of course he was only kidding. "A girl! Why would you want to be a girl?" asked Denver. "Because girls are smarter than boys, that's why," Ronnie replied. "Boys run faster than girls," said Denver, as he struggled to make sense of Ronnie's words. "So what! That doesn't mean *nothing*!" shouted Ronnie in reply. "Anyway, I ran a race with Megan and she beat me." "Megan Morgan beat *you*? Megan Morgan couldn't beat anybody," Denver said. But all Ronnie would say in response to Denver's argument was, "I've made up my mind. I'm going to be a girl!" The three children did not, could not, believe him. It was just a joke. It had to be a joke. It wasn't possible for a boy to become a girl even if he really wanted to. No way! Ronnie never had the satisfaction of assuming a role he could be comfortable in.

No less horrendous to the primary-age boys was the androgynous—or "gynandrous"—idea of a boy playing with dolls. When the song "William's Doll" from the record *Free to be You and Me* was played to children in grades one through three, the boys crawled under their desks and hid under coats on the coat rack to demonstrate their objection to and rejection of William, the small boy on the record who wanted a doll to hug and hold and give a bottle to. William's friends were embarrassed for him and taunted him as one way of discouraging him from pursuing his quest for a doll. His father tried to distract him from his unmanly desire for a doll by giving him a baseball and glove, a basketball, and a badminton set. William loved the gifts and was good at playing all of the games, but, he said, he would trade them all gladly for a doll he could love and care for and put to bed when day was through. William got his doll when his grandmother came to visit. She explained to William's father that some day William would be a father and that his experience in caring for his doll would help him when he had to care for his child.

The Pine Hill boys were painfully embarrassed for William. His behavior was an affront to them, still so unsure of their own status as men and struggling painfully to distance themselves from "babies" and "sissies," whether they were girls or unmanly boys like William. Babies and baby dolls belonged in the girls' world and a boy like William brought that world dangerously close to their own; they could be guilty by association. (Several years later the third-grade boys could hear this record without experiencing trauma.) Boys at Pine Hill did, as a matter of fact, play with dolls, but they were not baby dolls. The kind of doll William on the record wanted and eventually got was a baby doll. The kinds of dolls Pine Hill boys admitted to playing with were G.I. Joe dolls, Bionic Man dolls, and all the other adult male dolls engaged in dangerous or scientific pursuits. Many of these dolls were useful in playing war-strategy games popular with third-grade boys. "I have a whole lot of them," one second-grade boy said of this kind of doll. No role problems there. This was macho stuff.

Among the girls the doll issue was almost as sensitive as among boys. In the sense that dolls were something to hug and hold against one's body and give a bottle to, dolls were associated with babyhood. A very young boy or girl—that is, a child younger than a first-grader—might carry such a doll around not so much as a toy to play with as a soft object to comfort himself/herself with. The accusation, then, that girls played with dolls was not so much an attack on the mother role as on immaturity. No other put-down by boys carried the same invidious meaning as their taunt that girls must be babies because they played with baby dolls, a toy for babies. Girls were quick to catch the implication of inferiority. They resented it.

The girls defended themselves from the boys' put-downs by insisting that they did *not* like dolls, did *not* play with dolls, and, indeed, "wouldn't take one if it was given to me." In rebuttal to the boys' insistence that girls, like other babies, played with dolls, one first-grade girl said, "I don't play with dolls. I like to play ball and do all the things boys do outside." First-grader Terri, when asked if she played with dolls replied defensively, "Un-un! N-E-V-E-R! I play cowboys and Indians. We have a fort in the woods. I go there and play with the boys." Second-graders Paula and Jackie reluctantly admitted that they did play with dolls under some circumstances, such as when they role-played an adult mother and a small baby was needed.

Most girls, however, were uncomfortable with the subject of dolls. Here is what third-graders Elaine, Laura, and Elizabeth had to say about dolls: "Dolls, ugh!" responded Laura when the subject of dolls was brought up. "Boys are crazy to think girls like dolls. Dolls are stupid. Dolls are dumb." But it was Elizabeth who coined the word that gave the lie to the boys' accusations. "Dolls are stupidious!" Laura admitted that she did not understand why she felt so resistant to being identified with dolls. "I don't know why but I just want to get rid of my dolls. I told my mom, 'Mom, I want you to get rid of these dolls.' She said, 'Keep them so that you can give them to your own kids someday.' I hate that!"

"My grandmother gave me this doll that I have," said Elaine, "and I told her, 'I'm not going to take it,' and she said, 'Take it!' so I took it and I wrapped it up and gave it to Lorrie and Jane. I hate dolls! I couldn't stand one if I saw one." Now that they had made their feelings about dolls known, the girls began to chant in unison the taunt, "Boys like dolls! Boys like dolls!" Thus it was that at Pine Hill one of the battles of the sexes was fought out over the doll issue, an issue that brought underlying hostilities out into the open, with boys accusing girls and girls accusing boys of playing with a toy meant for babies.

Winning and Losing: Female Style

By any measure the proper perspective for both girls and boys at Pine Hill on the subject of winning was that, of course, it was fun to win. But there was a difference. Winning and losing had serious consequences for boys, while for girls the pleasure of winning or the disappointment of losing was not a life-and-death matter. If boys were to be accepted by their peers they *had* to win; they *had* to be first at least some of the time. The girls, of course, liked to be first as much as the boys did, and if the teacher conferred a first-place position on them—that of line leader, for example—they would fight to retain that honor. But among girls there was no structured group of peers watching and judging a girl's performance. Winning wasn't everything. A girl might even, if the occasion arose, let someone else win, as Sonya once did.

When Laura and Sonya entered the relay race in the annual field-day event, Laura had little hope of winning. With other girls in their class they had practiced daily and Sonya had always won. But Laura thought she would have fun anyway, so she had entered the race. However, on the day of the sports event it was Laura and not Sonya who won the blue ribbon. Laura could not believe her good luck. "When I signed up for that race I knew I'd be running against Sonya. I kept saying to myself, 'If I try a little harder maybe I can beat her,' and I did." Sonya, who had taken the second-place ribbon, said, "I let her win. She never beats me so I let her win the race." Laura looked at Sonya with affection and admiration. "That was really nice. I didn't know you were going to do that," she said. Future events in the upper elementary grades showed that it was questionable that Sonya had "let" Laura win the race, for long-legged Laura emerged as the all-school running champion in competition with both boys and girls. But her graceful acceptance of Sonya's claim to having "let" Laura win clearly showed that girls were under far less pressure to prove themselves than were boys. A boy who had claimed that he had "let" another boy win first place, thus challenging the winner's right to the first-place position, would have had to fight to validate his claim.

For boys the essence of the game was winning. For girls the point of the game was to have fun even when losing. Thus second-grader Debbie was able to tell Brian during a card game, "It doesn't matter who wins. It's just fun to play." Brian could not remotely agree. If he did not win it was because others had cheated or they had looked at his cards. Another interesting episode took place when second-graders Stephanie, Lewis, Dennis, and Linda were playing a board game during their free time in the classroom. Stephanie had taken charge of the game since there were decisions to be made that required a leader and she had strong leadership ability. She went beyond her role, however, to tell the other three children when it was their turn to play, how far to move their markers on the board, and what their cards told them to do. When Lewis moved his marker in the wrong direction, she scolded, "That's going back, Dumb Ox. Your card says, 'take another turn' so take another turn, Dumb Ox." Lewis ignored Stephanie's insulting epithet. Her guidance had put him ahead of the other players in the game, and he was far less interested in her opinion of him than in the fact that he was winning. "I'm going to win! I'm going to win!" he shouted with glee. "Oh, yeah, that will take a miracle," Stephanie scoffed as she turned over her next card and found it was a picture of a bride. "It's a good thing I got this one," she said. "A bride! That's what girls are supposed to get." But the bride card did not help Stephanie win the game. The boys won. "We won! We won!" Dennis and Lewis shouted as they took this opportunity to roll over one another on the floor. Stephanie was philosophical about her loss. It did not occur to her to diminish Lewis's pleasure by reminding him of her role in his winning. "Well, the game was fun even if I did lose." It had been no disgrace to lose. She had even enjoyed the game. She had drawn the bride card.

In such an unpressured world, in such a world of options, the girls did not have to avenge themselves; they did not have to attack the establishment. It was on their side. For girls, the prison bars were erected only gradually.

Becoming a Woman

Intense relationships that were analogous though not identical to those of boys came somewhat later for girls—that is, in the fourth grade rather than the third. The differences in sex-role socialization between boys and girls thus became especially marked in the fourth grade.

With their primary years behind them, options in the girls' world narrowed. They were no longer permitted the freedom to choose to be tomboys or ladies. They were now almost ten years old, and the new role model called for them to be as unlike boys as possible. Boys had begun the process of distancing themselves from the female world in first grade; girls began the process of distancing themselves from the boys' world in fourth grade. Boys had learned early to say that they hated girls who conformed to the feminine role, and adults expressed concern about girls like Tracey, who showed no inclination whatsoever to trade her position on the boys' ball team for a sidelines seat with the less sports-minded girls. They wondered aloud if Tracey would ever take her place in the adult world as a wife and mother.

Androgynous girls like Tracey had never had close ties to the teacher. Now, in the fourth grade, the other girls also began to distance themselves from teachers and to seek support from girlfriends rather than from adults. As young primary-age girls they had welcomed into their games anyone who wanted to play, but in fourth grade, as the pressures to conform to the stereotype for the female sex-role were intensified, they formed best-friend liaisons with only one other girl. As they entered into the best-friend relationship they pledged undying devotion to one another. These relationships they were sure would last forever.

The process of transferring from teacher orientation to peer orientation led to the first evidence of the kind of status differentiation among the girls that was so common among the boys. In this instance beauty was the key. The prettier the girl, the higher her status in the group, though being a good student and/or having a pleasing personality also helped. Less attractive girls had to settle for girls like themselves as best friends so that the basis of their bonding was often their resentment of the more attractive girls, whom they often referred to as "stuck up" or "acting big." This bonding in best-friend relationships generated considerable friction among the girls in the classroom. Best friends shared secrets that they would tell no one else, although they made a point of letting other girls know that they had secrets to share. Best friends were inseparable and they hoarded unto themselves as much of one another's time and affection as possible during the school day.

The "best-friend" relationship was prototypical of passionate love. It was a kind of apprenticeship for the mature male-female relationship of adulthood. It was intense, exclusive, demanding. Best friends wrote and exchanged notes in which they proclaimed their love and eternal friendship. Many of these notes were written on the electric typewriter in my office. The contents had a monotonous sameness about them. "Dear Sonya, you are my best friend and you always will be. I am very glad that you are my best friend. Love, Megan." While this letter was typical of the kinds of messages they wrote to one another, at more intense moments they would write as Regina did, "Dear Elizabeth, You are my best friend and we will always be best friends forever. We will be best friends and never be apart. Love, Regina."

For most of the girls the process of choosing and being chosen as best friend was a relatively simple one: girls who lived in the same neighborhoods and had played together for years simply gravitated toward one another. But for three of the girls—all exceptionally beautiful, all outstanding students—the process of breaking old ties with teachers and entering into an exclusive, overly possessive relationship with a best friend created a conflict that was to last throughout all of the fourth and into part of the fifth grade. Laura and Donna both sought to claim Elaine as best friend, and when she did not or would not commit herself to either girl, they entered into a struggle to control her that was as bitter as any between two women fighting over one man or two men over one woman. Both girls wooed Elaine with all the resources available to them. When Laura invited Elaine to accompany her family on a trip to a favorite amusement park, Donna countered by inviting her on a family camping trip. In this way Elaine enjoyed a considerable amount of "wining and dining" by the two girls and their families.

Elaine's ability to walk a middle line between Laura and Donna generated different responses in the two girls. Laura was gentle and loving, and I often found her crying in the school halls or on the playground because, "Donna took Elaine away from me. She told Elaine a lot of lies about me and now Elaine doesn't want to play with me anymore." She might have been able to accept the ménage-à-trois the girls' mothers and teachers tried to arrange, but not Donna. Donna had an iron will, and she was prone to telling others how to live their lives. "I don't want Laura playing with us. Elaine is my friend now and she doesn't like Laura anymore," she told adults who attempted to bring some harmony into the situation. Donna's possessiveness vis-à-vis Elaine extended even to the classroom, where she often attempted to answer questions the teacher directed to Elaine. On one occasion when Donna, as usual, had made a unilateral decision about what she and Elaine would do on a classroom project, Elaine tried to be assertive. "You're always first," she said, referring to the decision-making process that went into the assignment. "Sometimes I'd like to be first." Donna was obliging. "Oh, do you want to be first? You *can* be first if you want to." Pleased but not wanting to offend Donna, Elaine said, "Well, I don't want to be first all of the time, but I'd like to be first some of the time."

To regain her leadership role, as well as to placate Elaine, Donna said,"Well, the reason I always go first is because it's easier that way. If I have an idea and I ask you if you have an idea and you tell me your idea, then we have to discuss my idea and your idea and we just waste a lot of time. But if you want to be first you can be first. You can be first the next time." Elaine was happy with the solution. She never did get to be first in any situation she shared with Donna, but she would have admitted that life with Donna was never dull, for she was inventive, creative, and could always think of interesting things for them to do.

When Elaine, perhaps occasionally weary of having every detail of her life directed by Donna, slipped back into a relationship with the easier-to-live-with Laura, Donna retaliated against Laura by putting gum between the pages of her notebooks, putting tacks on her chair, and sending her anonymous letters threatening her life and claiming that everyone in their class hated Laura because she was mean and ugly. In spite of efforts to bring the girls together, the conflict remained unresolved until fifth grade, when boys entered the picture.

Even as the girls talked and fantasied about their undying love and friendship, they also talked and fantasied about the "cute, handsome, adorable" boys in their class, of being married, and of having children of their own. Marriage was still hugs and kisses, walking hand-in-hand, sharing secrets, sharing dreams, and keeping the world out; marriage was, in fact, another version of the best-friend relationship. The reality of hearing boys say, "Girls, ugh!" and "I hate girls," of being told to play their own games and leave boys' games alone, of hearing boys laugh whenever any mention was made of domestic chores and insist that scrubbing and cooking were "girl's work," never impinged on their romantic ideal of a boy who would be as loving and supportive of them as their own best friend was. They had entered into their own "I hate boys" era, but their new aversion to having their names publicly linked with those of boys did not diminish their romantic notion of adult love and marriage, possibly with one of the boys now in their classroom.

The girls themselves seemed to have considerable insight into the function of the best-friend relationship as preparation for later boy-girl relationships. Here, for example, is what three fifth-grade girls wrote about it:

> When you get older you can share things with the opposite sex because you are both mature then and you can understand things about one another. But when you are young, a person of the same sex is a better friend because you experience more of the same things. Since your body is more or less in the same shape as another person of the same sex your girlfriend understands what you are talking about. (Donna)

> I think that when a girl is young she needs a person of the same sex to be her friend and to share her personal thoughts with. When a girl is older she can understand the thoughts of the opposite-sex because she is more mature then. It is better for boys and girls to have personal relationships when they are older but at our age girls share personal thoughts with the same sex we are because our bodies are in the same shape. (Elaine)

> I believe that many persons from the age of eleven to fourteen cannot have a person of the opposite sex to be their friend in the same way that a person of the same sex can be their friend. This is true because most persons in that age group are not fully mature because we are still young and we cannot talk about many things with persons of the opposite sex. It would be nice if we were mature but in most cases we are not. Love and friendship with a boy can teach girls many things but at our age we still need someone of our own sex because our bodies are the same. (Megan)

When the focus of relationships came to be open, direct, girl-boy relationships, Pine Hill girls no longer felt the need to have an exclusive relationship with one other girl. By sixth grade the only relationships that could be termed exclusive came to be the girlfriend-boyfriend dating relationships, and even those were flexible and constantly changing affairs.

This, then, was the second curriculum in action. The adult world did well in defining its contents and the boys and girls themselves, with no difficulty, did well in learning it and in teaching it to one another. But there was a lot more to sex-role socialization. And this was, by adult default, a do-it-yourself kind of learning.

PART THREE

The Third Curriculum: Self-Taught Sex Education

·8·

FUN AND GAMES IN THE PRIMARY GRADES

Although there were many opponents to sex education in the schools who argued that sex education belonged in the home, there were not many parents who knew when or how to supply it. Even the anatomical and physiological facts were difficult to discuss, let alone the emotional concomitants. As a woman once said, "It's too autobiographical." So, while the adults hemmed and hawed, the children went about learning and experimenting on their own, careful to protect the frightened adult world from the facts of life. They indulged the adult world's need for ignorance, all the while garnering what they could from whatever source they could to expand on their personal observations. They found ways to circumvent adult scrutiny and allay suspicion. They had learned very early, for example, that they would be rebuked if found playing "doctor," so rather than ceasing to engage in such activities, they found ways to hide them from surveillance. Under a multitude of pretexts they felt and touched one another without arousing the suspicion of watchful adults. That was why my notes were relatively sparse.

Possibly because mothers of boys were more wary about their sons' sexuality—or more fearful of it—than were the mothers of girls, it was the girls of Pine Hill who were in charge of the first "lessons" of the third curriculum. They skillfully managed, for example, the House game played by first-grade girls and boys, as well as all the chasing, hugging, and kissing games that took place on the playground. Mothers dismissed with a smile their small sons' stories of being chased on the playground and kissed by girls. Five-, six-, and seven-year-old girls were not threats to any boy. When girls were sexually aggressive, adults were indulgent or pretended not to see. Parents could be generous when a very young girl kissed a boy of the same age. Such an act could even be considered "cute."

My notes revealed several stages or "grades" in the children's sex-education curriculum, which, though not as clear-cut as those in the first and second curricula, did succeed one another in a structured sequence. When I put them in rough order they appeared to be: (1) House; (2) Look and See; (3) Show and Tell; (4) Chase, Catch, and Kiss; (5) Girlfriend-Boyfriend; and, of course, (6) Fucking, discussed in chapter 9.

House

The game of "doctor" was not played at Pine Hill even by kindergarten children. It may have been played at home, although this was one game parents were likely to be on the lookout for and to discourage early on. So there were neither doctors nor patients in the primary grades. But there were fathers and mothers and children. Playing in the doll's corner in kindergarten was easily carried over in first grade to playing "house," where other children took the place of dolls. Though this game made Father only a silent partner and gave Mother all the good lines, it was popular with both sexes. It offered them the chance for almost unlimited physical contact. On one occasion, for example, first-graders Christine and Tony were chosen by classmates and friends to play Mother and Father. Christine busied herself at feeding the children, driving them to school and to music lessons, and cleaning the house; finally she called to them that it was time to go to bed. The children did not want to go to bed, so Christine chased them—boys as well as girls—around the classroom until, one by one, she caught them, spanked them—thus providing the children with rewarding physical contact—and put them to bed. Then, with a final word of warning to "stay there," she left them to join Tony, who had been sitting quietly on a chair in the "living room" all of this time. So far, all of this had been quite acceptable to the teacher. Together Christine and Tony then linked hands and crept quietly behind the large blackboard that hid the coat room from the view of the rest of the classroom and kissed and kissed.

This went beyond the limits of the second curriculum. When the teacher noticed that Christine and Tony were missing, she went to look for them. Their giggles and their feet sticking out from under the coats revealed their hiding place. She asked them what they were doing. "Playing house," they replied. "Let's play house in the classroom where I can watch you," she suggested. Sensing that something was wrong, they looked quite sheepish and separated. Some things that Mother and Father did were all right to imitate and could—indeed had to—be kept out in the open. But certain other things had to be camouflaged or kept secret.

Look and See

The second stage in the third curriculum was reached when the children began to have access to books and pictures that considerably enhanced their resources. Since one of the earliest forms of looking and seeing—the doctor game—was forbidden, a surrogate was found in pictures. The words "look" and "see" were among the first words they had learned from their primers, and now they could incorporate looking and seeing into their own curriculum. There were many more things than Spot to look at and see. The library became an important resource. At Pine Hill this could be called the *National Geographic*, or voyeuristic, stage.

The Pine Hill children displayed the usual interest of children in the female breast. Even in first grade they would search the pages of the *National Geographic*—the one sure source of photographs of the naked breast available—looking for the pictures that would help them visualize the breasts that might serve them as a pillow but that were always hidden from view. Giggling children shared their "finds" through a network of friends, who shared them with other friends until every child in the school had thumbed his or her way through pages of animals, birds, and fully attired people to find the women naked to the waist. If they looked at nothing else in the *National Geographic*, the magazine helped them understand parts of the female body that adults would not show them. The *National Geographic* did not show them pictures of the naked penis, nor did they expect to find such pictures, for at a very early age they knew the inflexible rule that genitals were to be kept under cover, where they would not offend others. Little girls who wore dresses were admonished to "sit like ladies" so that they would not expose their panties to the gaze of curious boys. But the boys of Pine Hill had their own strategies for looking at girls' panties and beyond. Boys who chased girls on the playground often attempted to pull down their panties, as much, to be sure, for the screams of protest from girls as for what they could see.

As the boys grew older they engaged in the ultimate defiance of establishment rules when they invaded the girls' restroom. It had both an inside and an outside door that opened on the playground and was unlocked during free play periods. Punishment by teachers and parents was not sufficient to discourage boys from entering the girls' restrooms from the outside door. Often a group of three or four boys would run screaming through the girls' restroom and out again before they could be stopped. Boys also pulled down the pants of other boys, and one third-grader was tormented by peers who made a practice of chasing him down the hill and out of sight of the playground aide, where they would pull his pants below his knees and tighten his belt so that he had to struggle a few minutes to get his pants back into place. Girls and boys alike seemed to enjoy the spectacle of a third-grade boy standing at the bottom of the hill in his shorts.

Show and Tell

In addition to voyeurism, a corresponding kind of exhibitionism was practiced by first-grade boys, who, with nothing of consequence to show, still took great delight in teasing little girls with the suggestion of a displayed penis. To get the effect they wanted they thrust their hands into their pants and then wiggled their fingers at girls through an open fly.

If the boys had little to show at that age, the girls had less. By fifth grade, however, as the girls began to mature, this kind of show-and-tell appeared among them also. At this time their bodies began to alert both the boys and the girls themselves that they were females. As soon as they had something to show, they played their counterpart to the show-and-tell game, "Snapsies." As breasts began to form on some of the girls, they began to wear "training" bras. Even the girls who were still "flat as pancakes" wore bras, as much to show themselves as to show others that they had the potential for breasts. Snapsies was not a new game but their approach to it was, for when the classroom was completely silent, one girl would pull the bra strap of another girl as far back as her outer clothing would permit and then release it so that it snapped loudly against the wearer's back. This produced loud laughing and prolonged stares at the chest of the girl whose bra had been snapped. The Snapsies game was considered fun and exciting. It showed and told, in effect, that the girls were becoming sexy.

The fifth-grade girls used other means to communicate the message about this new phase in their development. On one occasion, for example, Donna came into the library with a notebook clutched to her chest. "I'm going to have to carry this around all day," she confided to me. "Why?" I asked. "Look," she said as she quickly dropped her notebook from her chest and just as quickly replaced it. "What am I supposed to look at?" I asked. "Look again," she said as she lowered her notebook, this time for a longer period. "I'm so embarrassed. Have you got any ideas about what I can do so I don't have to keep this in front of me all day? I won't be able to get any work done." So slender and delicate that not even a small bump showed on her sweater, Donna had, nevertheless, begun to wear a bra and this morning had forgotten to put it on. By the middle of the morning she had managed to establish her claim to breasts with the people who counted, her peers, so she could put aside her notebook and get on with the affairs of the day. Her ploy had served its purpose.

Chase, Catch, and Kiss

First-grade boys chased the girls and, like Georgie Porgie, made them cry. But, unlike Georgie Porgie, they did not kiss the girls they chased. Instead, they teased them and hit them. One first-grader reported that his peers had put it to him quite bluntly, "You pee on a girl, you don't kiss her." The tradition of chasing girls to tease or hurt them was carried on throughout the school. On one occasion third-grade boys were chasing girls as they called out to them, "This is TTT Day." They told me later that the initials stood for "Texas Titty-Twister" day. They would grab whatever flesh they could on a girl's chest and twist it. The girls reported that while having their flesh twisted hurt a bit, it was "worth it." The game was fun.

Hitting a girl, peeing on a girl, chasing a girl to make her cry, twisting a girl's "titty" was not sexual play and did not arouse the concern of adults. This hostile kind of chasing was granted tacit approval by the second curriculum. It was loving, kissing, and touching in affectionate ways that were aberrations that had to be hidden from adult scrutiny. And this part of the third curriculum was controlled by girls, not boys.

From first through sixth grade, girls were, or were made to seem, the aggressors in this game, for while boys lived it and cooperated fully, they would disavow any part in it if questioned by adults. In the first and second grades the chasing game consisted of isolated "hit-and-run" incidents, but by third grade it was planned and cooperatively carried out by both sexes, although it was the girls who were expected to initiate the plans and execute them. At some time during the morning hours—usually at lunch—a girl would indicate to a boy that she would like to chase him on the playground. If he agreed, he would then make himself available to her and the chase would begin. The boy never stayed too far away from the girl, but when she caught him he would escape and the chase would begin again. So popular was this game that even when it interfered with their beloved ball game, there were times when all the Tent Club boys would, as a group, forego the ball game to participate in the chasing game.

Toward the end of second grade a new element was added to the chase, catch, and touch game. It now became a chase, catch, and kiss game. The rules accommodated themselves. The reward—or "punishment"—for the boy at the end of the chase was a kiss from the girl who had been permitted to catch him. Obedience to the rules was absolute. Mothers of second-grade boys reported from time to time that their sons would complain that girls in their class had chased them and kissed them while they had just stood still and taken their punishment. The boys sometimes wrote letters to the advice column of the school newspaper complaining, for example, that "there is this girl who likes me and she kisses me all the time. What should I do?" Kissing was a female game, something that girls initiated and controlled. There were no sexually aggressive males in the second grade at Pine Hill, no Rhett Butlers carrying their Scarlett O'Haras, kicking and screaming, into the boudoir. But no boy ever welched on his word to allow himself to be kissed if caught. No boy ever went to the teacher to complain. To forbid this game would have been futile, so no teacher or playground aide ever noticed a thing.

When I mentioned to the third-grade boys that a lot of kissing seemed to be going on at recess, they assumed that I meant the comment as a rebuke. Like their original forebear, they shifted the blame to the girls. They had not wanted to be chased or kissed, but the girls who chased them were too strong and powerful for them and they had to submit to their fate. Even the excluded boys who played with girls when they had nothing else to do felt compelled to explain that they were not responsible for all the kissing they were doing. "I'll tell you how she gets me into it," Ronnie once told me. "She chases me and I run. Then I get to a place where I can't run anymore. Like she chases me to the end of the hall and I'm trapped. Then she grabs me and kisses me." When I did not scold or rebuke him, he added as an afterthought, "Man, that was fun!" Permitted the freedom to be honest with an adult—a freedom normally denied by the second curriculum—he allowed me in. Way in. Even the Tent Club boys, once they understood that I was not critical of this game, changed their tune. As a member of the Tent Club I could be trusted, and I could expect honesty from them. Billy and Chad even offered me a "piece of the action." "If you'll come outside at Free Play today we'll chase you," they said. This was not an instance of boys chasing a girl. I was older, much older, than the combined ages of the two boys. They knew I could have no reason for wanting to chase and kiss them so they would agree to bend their principles a bit so that I could take part in the fun.

When the principal of Pine Hill was alerted to the kissing that was occurring in the hallways and in the library as well as on the playground, he groaned, "I'm running a kissing academy, not an elementary school." Not until a substitute teacher took over the fifth grade for several days did the boys and girls get their first chance to kiss and kiss and kiss in the classroom. She was young enough to remember what it was like to be an elementary-school child and inexperienced enough to think that she could change their kissing habits by showing them that adults did not frown on kissing per se but that there was a time and place for everything. She would, therefore, let them kiss in the classroom under supervision. One day during their free play period she suggested that the fifth-graders play "Spin the Bottle" in the classroom instead of going outside for the ball games. The experiment boomeranged. With such a nonjudgmental adult in charge, the game was a huge success and the children insisted on playing it whenever they had free time. Soon everyone in the school—child and adult—knew that the fifth-graders were playing "Spin the Bottle." Adults in the school began to worry about the image of the school in the community. It took a major effort on the part of their regular classroom teacher to persuade the boys and girls that kissing was not a school-approved activity and could not take place in the classroom. But there were other places where it could—the library, for example.

In the fifth grade the boys and girls began to gravitate more and more to the library as a place to meet and kiss. One particularly golden opportunity arose when the librarian had to go to a meeting and the library was left dark and unattended. After some preplanning, a group of fifth-graders asked permission to go to the library to work on reports, and since they were mature, reliable youngsters who could be counted on not to hurt another child or themselves, they were permitted to go. They found that a group of sixth-graders was already there working on reports, although the lights had not been turned on and reading was therefore difficult. Donna sat at a table beside sixth-grader Craig, and in no time both fifth-graders and sixth-graders were chatting about boy-girl affairs. In the midst of the chatter Chad challenged Donna and Craig to prove themselves. He would give them a quarter for every minute they could hold a kiss without breaking apart. They accepted. For two minutes they maintained mouth-to-mouth contact before their laughter and the need to breathe broke them apart. Chad paid the fifty cents. Craig accepted with a promise to buy Donna a present. She refused to take the money. "I don't know why but I just don't want it," she said. She had not, like him, defined the event as a test or challenge.

Boyfriend and Girlfriend

There was a world of difference between a "boyfriend" and a boy friend, between a "girlfriend" and a girl friend. "Boyfriend" or "girlfriend" was a special kind of status and it was different for girls and for boys. The terms were used differently, reflected different kinds of relationships.

For the boys "girlfriends" were necessary adjuncts for the macho role. Having them—lots of them—was part of the Super-Jock test. As early as the second grade, having a "girlfriend" was essential to the completion of the macho model the boys were in the process of developing for themselves. Boys/men were expected to be attractive, even irresistible, to girls/women, and second-grade boys adopted this aspect of the male role with considerable zest. They teased one another about their "girlfriends" and about being in love, emphasizing the charges with slaps on the back and loud giggles. "Candy's Brian's 'girlfriend.' He's in love with her," the second-grade boys told me. "And Sean's in love with Carrie." They fell laughing against one another. They were tentatively building up the Don Juan reputations that depended on the cooperation of girls. It was girls and only girls who could validate a boy's claim to having passed the Don Juan test required by the second curriculum but achieved by means of the third. Alerting others to their sexual attractiveness to girls was important in establishing one's claim to having passed the Super-Jock test. It was prototypical of adolescent "scoring" with girls. In the third grade the requirements of the Don Juan test had become more stringent and, like other activities, highly competitive. Boys bragged surreptitiously to one another about the number of times they had been caught and kissed by any one girl. "Megan caught me and kissed me a hundred times," reported Derek to his friends, and they congratulated him on his success. He did not repeat Denver's mistake and openly confess to his complicity in the chasing and kissing game he had played with Megan. "Girlfriends" were only a means to a competitive end. Thus, when asked if they had girl-friends the Tent Club boys, said, "YECCH!"

In the formation of their Don Juan image, the boys could also adopt the persona of Knights in White Armor protecting ladies fair. Thus when Denver threatened to beat Megan up, Derek issued a counterthreat. If Denver laid just one finger on Megan, he would beat Denver up. Such protection of girls had the effect not only of enhancing machismo but also of excluding girls from the male world, where they could get hurt being around such rough boys. Girls were necessary adjuncts to boys in sex games, but in the macho world of real men they could not be tolerated as either play pals or as friends.

"Boyfriends" played quite a different role in the lives of the girls than did "girlfriends" in the lives of boys. Second-grade girls did tease one another about having "boyfriends," but the context was not, as among boys, competitive. The girls did not need "boyfriends" as adjuncts to their female role. "Boyfriends" had to do with being in love, and this was serious business. Love was the stuff marriages were made of. Chasing boys on the playground, catching and kissing them, rubbing against their genitals, these were, they vaguely sensed, what being a housewife was ultimately all about. As second-grader Stephanie noted, brides were what girls were supposed to be by way of the boys they caught and married. That boys said they hated girls and did not want girls playing their games was not at all relevant to their sex plans, for in this activity girls were not only wanted, they were actually needed.

Third-grade girls spent endless amounts of time fantasizing about "boyfriends" and marriage. Any gesture of appreciation shown to them by boys—the lending of a pencil or an eraser—was viewed as a display of personal interest and would be eagerly discussed with other girls. They talked of engagement rings, wedding dresses, being a housewife, and having children of their own. Third-grader Maureen bragged to her friends that she had a "boyfriend" from another school who had given her a diamond engagement ring. She explained that her mother would not let her wear it to school because it was valuable and she might lose it. If other girls did not believe her, they did not want to admit it. An engagement ring, like a first-grade boy's ability to play foxy football, was conceivable even when not entirely believable, because it fit the second-curriculum model for the female sex-role.

Third grade was to be the last year either the boys or the girls would admit to any sex activities in their self-devised sex-education curriculum. Thereafter such activities had to be kept sub rosa.

·9·

GAMES OF CHANCE

The third curriculum had been fairly easy to ignore in the primary grades. It became more difficult to avoid in the fourth grade and beyond. The boys and girls began to talk in whispers about their games. They became increasingly embarrassed to have their names publicly linked with the names of opposite-sex peers. The sixth-grade teacher remarked that his students refused even to sit beside one another or to do anything together. Their sex games, always played away from adult eyes or in a deceptive manner to allay adult fears, had now gone even further underground.

In the case of boys, learning how to "make it" with the girls was basic. They knew that among older boys and men one was graded on his "scoring" record. "Making it" was a rule of the male world that could not be openly taught but that all the boys considered essential. As one man put it, "You are told at an early age to get your sex when you can and where you can and not to ask questions."[1] Sixth-grade boys reported being told by fathers that they had to be able to "make it" with girls they dated and that at age twelve they were too young to make the most of a dating relationship. One sixth-grade boy told his peers that he had learned all about the "facts of life" when he was nine years old. When I asked him what the facts of life were, he said, "fun in bed." His remark was accompanied by exchanged punches and giggles from peers. Another sixth-grade boy remarked that "A girlfriend is someone you see everyday. A girl you see just once in a while is for . . . well, you know." He raised his eyebrows, looked up toward the ceiling, and made hand gestures to convey to his peers his sophistication in sexual matters. Third-grader Ronnie had tried to communicate the same message when he bragged that boys enjoy kissing games more than girls because, "well, you know!" If boys were perceived as the beneficiaries of sex play, they were also the ones who were blamed when these activities came to the attention of adults. Girls had to be protected; boys did not.

Quite independent of either best-friend or girl-boy relationships was the unstructured group sharing by the girls of what knowledge they could glean about their bodies and about the hazards they were learning they were exposed to. Many were beginning to find their little-girl, almost neuter bodies turning into female bodies without forewarning or preparation. Some of the changes were welcome. Breasts became a competitive ploy, as in the race to see who would be the first to wear a "training" bra.

The adult opposition to sex education in the school extended even to such factual, nonmoral phenomena as menstruation. For some girls adolescence arrived before the adult world was ready for it. By the fifth grade the school had to be ready to help a girl through her first period. The girls looked to one another and not to adults in the school or to parents to provide them with information even about menarche, let alone about sexuality.

Throughout elementary school, same-sex peers continued to play an important role in providing information about the biological changes occurring in their bodies. But there was another kind of sex education that same-sex peers could not teach one another. It had to do with relationships with the other sex. And here the deficiency in their education was even greater than it was with regard to the strict physical facts.

In the fourth grade the media rushed in to fill the vacuum created by adult avoidance of sex education. Television and the print media together supplied more about the relations between the sexes than many of the girls could handle. And same-sex groups supplied the "classroom discussion" that fixed the lessons. This was a darker part of the third curriculum.

The girls learned that the male world consisted of more than benign fathers, brothers, and obstreperous but controllable classroom peers. There were sinister men who violated women. There was rape. And as a result of rape, or even love, there was pregnancy and childbirth or often, abortion. These were issues that exerted a kind of fascination for them. They engaged in absorbing discussions of them. They shared their scanty information, abundant misinformation, and attitudes that had been formed at home and at church. Rape, childbirth, abortion—these were realities of their female world and could conceivably happen to them. Parents and other adults were, of course, unacceptable as sources of information. Adults, they said, always giggled when they attempted to discuss sex with them. Peers took these issues seriously. It was from this source, then, rather than from parents, school, or church, that most of this frightening component of their sex education came.

I did not meet one sixth-grade girl who did not know that girls their age could be raped. They had heard of twelve-year-old girls being raped on the school playground in after-school hours. They

had heard of women being raped in laundry rooms in their apartment buildings. They had heard of women who had been raped in
the security of their own homes by men posing as workmen or deliv-
ery men. For months the local newspapers and television had been
full of stories of two elementary-school girls who had disappeared
from a local shopping center and were never again heard from. Rape,
or worse, was suspected. Local police visited schools in the area to
warn children not to speak to strangers. And, while boys could also
be raped, it was stressed that it was the girls who were to be particularly careful. It was girls who were preyed upon by men. The rapist
presented to them by police was a degenerate stranger, though the
girls knew this was not always true. Peggy, a beautiful red-headed
woman who starred on their favorite afternoon television soap op-
era, had been raped by Mac Howard, a man she knew and trusted.
The girls tried to make some sense out of this mindless violence, and
they turned to same-sex peers to help them understand.

Laura had been visiting relatives in another state when the rape of
Peggy had taken place, so she had had to ask, "What is her name?
The woman who got raped, I mean." "Peggy, the woman with the
beautiful red hair," she was told. "Who raped her?" "Mac Howard."
"How could he do that to her? They were friends," Laura cried. Not
one girl had a ready answer. How, indeed, could a friend rape a
friend?

Nor could the girls understand Peggy's ambivalence toward the
unborn child that had resulted from the rape. "First she said she
wanted it and then she said she didn't want it. When she said she
wanted it she said she could take care of it herself. I guess she can't
make up her mind but if she decides to get rid of it, that's abortion!"
declared Donna. She had said, "That's abortion!" exactly as she
would have said, "That's murder." Elizabeth agreed. "Abortion is
like ending a life that's supposed to come. Would you want to die
even before you had a chance to do anything? Even to *get out*?"
"Abortion," said Elaine, "is as bad as letting the baby be born and
then knifing it in the throat. If you were a baby you wouldn't want to
be dead."

Only Tracey dissented from this popular point of view. She had
listened quietly as her friends expressed their strong aversion to
abortion, and when she thought they were through discussing their
feelings, she said, "An unborn baby doesn't know what life is so how
is it going to know what death is?" Shocked silence greeted Tracey,
and then Donna recovered enough to ask, "Would you want to be
dead?" Tracey leaned back on her chair and said in a firm voice,
"The baby doesn't know what is happening to it because the baby
can't think, dummy. Do you think the baby is in its mother's stomach

saying, 'Mama, Mama, don't kill me?' if the mother says she is going to have an abortion? The baby can't think because the baby hasn't lived, dummy."

Tracey's intelligence and performance as a student were highly respected by her peers and they had no evidence with which to refute or support her argument. The heavy silence was broken by Brenda, who said, "I know a woman who got raped in the laundry room in my apartment building." "Did they catch the guy who did it?" asked Elizabeth. Now the conversation was on safe ground. They could all agree that rape was a terrible crime and that it happened to girls and women.

The Ultimate No-No

Parents and other adults argued endlessly and volubly about sex education in the schools—what, when, where, by whom. "They're too young to learn about sex," argued some adults. "It encourages too much experimentation." "They don't need it yet." "It tells them more, much more, than they want to know." Anything to avoid or at least postpone the issue. Meanwhile the children had been providing their own sex education, one that had been proceeding grade by grade, from kindergarten on, pari-passu with the academic and sex-role curricula. When the boys and girls entered fourth grade at about the age of ten, the third curriculum began to take a new, more focused course.

The bottom line in the second curriculum was: do not have sexual relations with one another. The written and unwritten rules converged to emphasize this point. Adults might turn away from the sight of young children hugging and kissing, or even permit it under proper adult surveillance. But intercourse, never. Especially never for girls. The children knew that something or other that men and women did was terribly secret. And they had a word for it, "fucking."

To the youngest of children the term "fucking" did not mean penetration but, rather, the rubbing together of genitals. Even with one's clothes on. Several years earlier in another school, I had taught a Head Start class in which there were over thirty four-year-old children, black and white, who would often climb unabashedly on top of one another and simulate sexual intercourse. When asked what they were doing, they would answer either that they were playing "Mommy and Daddy" or that they were "fucking," apparently synonymous terms in their minds. They learned soon enough from the many adults in the Head Start classroom that "fucking" was not approved of for young children, and that if they wanted to play the game they had to hide it from adult eyes.

Even younger children sought to emulate adult sexual behavior. Thus, on trips to the Head Start community with a male anthropologist doing research, we heard a three-year-old girl recite a litany she had no doubt learned from adult females in her home. Patting her lips she began, "I'll give you this, Mr. Mays." Then she proceeded to pat her chest, stomach, and mons veneris as she repeated at each step the promise "I'll give you this, Mr. Mays." She had no idea what it was she was offering Mr. Mays; only that it was something enticing to men.

In another incident a mother said that she had become uneasy when she heard smothered but continuous giggling coming from the fenced-in back yard where her seven-year-old daughter was playing with two nine-year-old girls. When she asked what they were doing they told her that they had been "fucking." She asked them how they did that and they told her that they had "rubbed" those "little things" against one another. She told the girls that the correct term for those "little things" was clitoris and that girls had a clitoris while boys had a penis. Her manner was matter-of-fact. The girls then asked if they could hurt themselves if they "fucked" in this manner. Such fears—that something "bad" might happen to children who fucked—were expressed only by girls in my experience.

I first became aware of these fears in very young girls some years earlier, when, in another school, I answered a knock at my door early one morning to find Cindy and Sara, both third-graders, standing there, Sara calm but Cindy upset, with tears streaming down her cheeks. Why was she crying? "Ms. Best, do you think I'm pregnant?" she asked between sobs. I assured her that she was not, but why did she ask? Because, she explained, she had been "fucking" in the tool shed behind a friend's house. "How do you do that?" I asked. "I take off my panties, he takes off his pants, and I sit on his lap." After my repeated assurances that Cindy could not possibly be pregnant, both girls told me with considerable excitement that fucking was fun; more fun than anything they had ever done. It made them feel "good." Cindy's fears had been aroused when Sara told her that there was a connection between fucking and pregnancy. Although many of the second- and third-grade boys and girls were, as I subsequently learned, meeting in the tool shed to engage in the rubbing together of genitals—which they called "fucking"—no boys ever expressed a fear of being harmed by this activity.

At Pine Hill "fucking" was a popular term both to be used against the establishment and to describe an activity itself. Parents of kindergarten children, usually boys, would express alarm when they learned that their five-year-olds had acquired a vocabulary of four-letter words, including fuck, that they used indiscriminately with peers and, on occasion, with adults. Older children in the school wrote "fuck" on their notebooks, papers, and the lavatory walls. "Fuck you" or "go fuck yourself" were common terms used to express anger or annoyance with peers. I never heard these terms used against teachers at Pine Hill, but when the children were out of earshot they might easily have said to a teacher who scolded them, "fuck you!"

The early onset of puberty in some girls caused teachers to be on the lookout for girls and boys who disappeared from sight on the playground. Of these girls teachers often said, tongue in cheek, "I hope we get her out of here [Pine Hill] before she becomes pregnant." Sixth-graders Caroline and Carlotta were two girls who caused considerable concern among the Pine Hill staff. Both were large, well-developed girls and both were more than casually interested in capturing the attention of boys. While it was accepted that both Caroline and Carlotta could conceive, the school staff felt reasonably certain that few of the boys could make it happen.

Adults and The Third Curriculum

The academic curriculum was designed and administered by highly professional adults who had studied for years what to include at what age and what to do when things went wrong in the learning process. The second curriculum also, though not as straightforward, was in the hands of adults, a wide range of adults, in fact, from those in the media to parents. But the part adults played in the third curriculum was one of disturbed and troubled evasiveness. They did not want their children to experience any part of sexual activity, so they ignored it as much as they could. Understandably so.

Teaching boys to be boys and girls to be girls was child's play compared to teaching boys and girls how to relate to one another in a loving but not exploitative way. And dealing with the physical aspects of such relationships, even those which were most innocent, could be traumatic for adults.

The teachers' hands were tied. School personnel could not become involved. To suggest to parents that their child was fucking in someone's tool shed or behind the hill might well lead to court action, to the teacher's being sued by the parents. A teacher who attempted to discuss the matter with one girl's mother was told to keep her hands off. Sometimes a teacher's intervention resulted in breaking up a boy-girl relationship on the basis of unfounded suspicions, as in the case of Ronnie and Carrie. The two second-grade cousins had been doing their homework together in the boy's bedroom until a teacher, suspecting that the children were doing more than reading and arithmetic every night, discussed her fears with the principal of the school, who arranged a conference with the children's parents, the teacher, and a medical doctor assigned by a local school board to such cases. It was explained to the parents that the closeness of the children's relationship could only lead to body contact, which would bring them harm.

The mother of a beautiful little girl who wore both her hair and her skirts so that they just reached the bottom of her buttocks wrote a note to the third-grade teacher ordering her to tell the boys in her class that it was "all right to look at Melanie and admire her" but not to touch her. Melanie's gyrations as she danced, her hair and skirts drawing attention to her panty-clad bottom, made it difficult for the teacher to provide the protection her mother requested.

Nor were fathers exempt from uneasiness in the presence of sex play, even among very small preschool children. The father of a two-year-old boy was deeply disturbed when he saw his son and a neighbor's two-year-old daughter hugging and kissing in his back yard. He attempted to stop the kissing by offering them a ball and suggesting, firmly, that they play with it. The children obediently took the ball and began to push it back and forth between them. Pleased with himself, the father returned to the house. Turning for one last look at the children, he saw the ball lying discarded on the grass and the children hugging and kissing. This time he did not intervene. But he did wonder why he thought he should. His discomfort was typical of the reactions of Pine Hill parents to any kind of contact between the sexes.

Mothers too often felt helpless. First-grader Adam's mother feared that her son had been playing doctor with first-grader Anne and told Anne's mother that the relationship must either be watched carefully—they must never be left alone in the playroom, for example—or stopped altogether. Preferably stopped. Sixth-grader Caroline's mother told the teacher, who wanted to discuss Caroline's behavior, that she could not tell her daughter what to do since she always used the old ploy, "You don't love me"; and now that Caroline was twelve years old she would do whatever she wanted to do anyway. Third-grader Cindy's mother never suspected that Cindy was "fucking" in the tool shed, but she did evince concern when Cindy's sixth-grade brother told her that he saw Cindy go into the woods with a group of boys. Cindy, who knew all about adult concerns, told her mother that the boys "made" her go to with them and "made" her take her panties off. Her mother called the police, who, after questioning

Cindy, reported that she was "the calmest child they had ever seen" under such circumstances. Their suggestions to Cindy's mother: give her a hot bath and put her to bed. The boys, on their side, when questioned by the police, admitted they had taken Cindy into the woods; they did not implicate her.

Third-grader Sara's mother also had recourse to the police. When she learned that Sara had been meeting a teen-age boy at a fort in the woods, she became suspicious. Although her doctor reassured her that Sara had not been penetrated, she asked the police to look into the matter. Sara's parents took strong measures to control her behavior. So strong, in fact, that Sara was eventually referred to social services as an abused child.

It was easy for a boy's mother to say that she was worried about one of the girls in his class who sat in a parked car on the school parking lot after dark, but it was impossible for her to imagine her own son—who played with girls in the bushes near a church—engaged in any kind of sexual activity. Even if she had been able to admit it, she would not have known what to do beyond the kind of action taken by Sara's parents—severe beatings—or Cindy's—calling in the police. There were no easy answers to sex at an early age.

PART FOUR

Stereotypes and Friendships

·10·

CLEARING THE DEBRIS

There was a growing uneasiness in the mid-seventies about the new sexual scene. It was a disquieting time. I was not pleased with the general path the children were following. The mores that were being inculcated in them had evolved in a past when most women were going to spend most of their lives bearing and rearing children in the household and most men were going to spend most of their lives in the work force supporting them. There was to be little contact between the sexes outside the family. Now millions of women, even wives and mothers, were streaming into the labor force. Women and men were going to be thrown into one another's company more and more. But only one pattern of relationships was being absorbed by the Pine Hill children: you either hated members of the other sex or you loved them. These children were not much better prepared to relate to one another than their parents' generation, whose attitude was succinctly expressed by Father Timothy, a small-town priest I had known in my childhood: "There is no such thing as a platonic relationship between the sexes."

Much influenced myself by the new intellectual currents sweeping through our society, I was not at all happy with the anachronistic patterns the children at Pine Hill were being trained into. I felt they had to be prepared for better relationships with one another; they had to have more options than hatred or—sexual—love. There had to be a middle ground. It had to be possible for boys and girls to meet, to enjoy one another, to share more than their bodies. I wanted to see if it was. I knew I could do nothing to mitigate what was coming to be known as an epidemic of teenage pregnancies. Nor could I revolutionize dating habits. The objectives I set for myself were more limited. I wanted to see what I could do with just one class—the new fourth-graders—to sidetrack the sexual emphasis during the three years left for them in elementary school. Was it possible for preadolescent boys and girls to become friends? Could precocious experimentation with sex be headed off?

I did not presume to believe I knew the answers. But I did know

129

that merely ignoring the relations between the sexes or chasing the subject underground, thereby endowing it with a fascinating mystique, was not an auspicious way to deal with it. It led to the conception of the relations between boys and girls, men and women, exclusively in terms of the forbidden physical sexuality. It greatly restricted the nature of contacts between the boys and girls. I knew I could not prevent the boys and girls from being attracted to one another, even if I had wanted to, which I did not. But I wondered if it were possible to show them that the relationship could be one of affectionate friendship rather than one of potential sexual intercourse.

In a school setting the best tools available to me, I concluded, were words, a reading teacher's stock-in-trade. I had had years of experience with the liberating effect of the "talking cure," the ability to verbalize all kinds of emotions. In dealing with children who needed special help it had always seemed to me important to show them how to put their problems into words, to get a handle on them by way of conversations with me. It occurred to me that if I could help the boys and girls talk about their relationships with one another, it might help them understand them. I was not going to have contact with them very much longer, and if I was going to undertake this effort the time was now.

In order to clear the way, it was essential that the children learn to see the world around them as it really was rather than seeing it through the distorting lens of the stereotypes acquired in the second curriculum. It was especially important for the boys to see the actual girls in their lives, who were busily and competently performing, rather than the passive, incompetent girls they saw in the textbooks, library books, and the media. At the same time, the boys had to see themselves and all other males in their lives through their own eyes rather than in terms of the male stereotypes. For the girls, the psychological work was less difficult, less painful. Indeed, whereas the boys had to tarnish their own image of superiority by reducing the male stereotypes to size, the girls had primarily to upgrade the stereotypes to recognize how much better they were than the stereotyped image of girls.

In assaulting the stereotypes I was not unaware of the hazards entailed. When reality was superior to the stereotypes, as in the case of girls, it was a positive gain to see reality. But when reality was inferior to the stereotype, what was the expected result? There was always the danger of debunking for its own sake. One had to distinguish between legitimate norms of behavior and misleading stereotypes. "Crime doesn't pay" expresses a norm against crime. Actually we know that sometimes crime pays handsomely. Heroes and heroines are often endowed with stereotypical virtues. Was there any value in deliberately playing up their faults? How does one deal with the idealized stereotypes in light of grim, often sordid, reality? Could it lead to confusion? Would the result of ridding them of the stereotypes that demanded so much of boys, limited the vision of girls, and separated the sexes into different worlds be worth the risks involved? I thought it would. We would bring their stereotypes into the light of day and confront them.

At Pine Hill the boys' image of men vis-à-vis women was nearly identical to that reported by Ruth Hartley in her study of sex-role socialization: "Men . . . must be able to protect women and children in emergencies; they have to have more manual strength than women; . . . they must get money to support their families. . . . In the family, they are the boss. . . . Compared with mothers, fathers are more fun to be with. . . ."[1]

In the course of our discussions on what it meant to be a man, I once asked what an adult man could do that the boys couldn't. Adult men, according to the media models, could get drunk, gamble, ride very fast in a motorcycle, ride a minibike, take part in drag races, and, to cap it all, men could be the boss. When the boys' attention was called to their own observations of real life, they were not so sure of themselves. Life did not always corroborate the media stereotype that men were the bosses. Sometimes they weren't. Chad expressed concern about whether or not he would actually be able to participate in the delightful male activities. "Probably my wife won't even let me drink or gamble," he mused. "Would you obey your wife if she said that you couldn't drink or gamble?" "Y-E-A-H!" He seemed astonished at my question. Of course he would obey his wife. Didn't everyone? I'm not sure he grasped the incongruity between the stereotypes and the reality.

The Psychological Work of Boys

But the boys' hardest psychological work had to do with reconciling their stereotypes of girls with reality. There were, for example, many girls in the school—Tracey, Julia, Megan, Terri, Laura, Sonya, and Regina—to name a few—who did not conform at all to the boys' stereotype for the feminine sex-role. The girls' androgynous behavior on the playground and in the classroom constantly challenged the stereotype, a situation that created a considerable amount of stress for the boys.

As early as first grade, there had been many girls who had said that the games they liked best were those "games you play outside like football." Nevertheless, six-year-old Brian, who knew nothing of anatomy or biology—and very little about football—could parrot one version of the stereotype: "Girls aren't hardly made for football." The rebuttal by girls, "Some girls are made for football," or even the plain fact that androgynous girls were notably successful on the boys' ball teams, had not been sufficient to convince Brian or any other boy. The two girls who sprang to their feet in rebuttal to Brian's dictum were not substituting one stereotype for another. They had said that *some* girls were as well made for football as boys, a fact that girls were successfully demonstrating on the playground every day. The boys were equally aware of the girls who played ball as well as boys, but they had difficulty making the psychological jump from what they heard and were supposed to believe to what they saw and knew to be true. The solution arrived at was a constant repetition of the stereotypes, as though the words erased the facts.

It was not only the actual behavior of the girls that confounded the stereotypes. Implicit in Brian's statement that girls were not made for football was the correlative notion that boys—*all boys*—were made for football. Still there were some boys, like third-graders Kenny and Edward, who did not care to play ball and were not good ball players. Since there was no ready explanation in the stereotypes for such nonmacho behavior, the boys disposed of the problem by disposing of those who did not conform; they rejected the sissies and banished them.

It was not, however, so easy to dispose of girls who played ball as well as or better than boys. A substitute stereotype was clearly in order. They supplied it. The new stereotype: "Boys have more fun playing ball." Jonathan supplied the emphasis, "Yeah, boys all the way." I challenged them. "If girls play all the games boys play and enjoy playing them, how can you say that boys have more fun than girls?" The differences had to be sharpened, to be made more in line with the stereotype.

The boys were equal to the occasion. "Because boys play rough," Chad told me, and his peers nodded in agreement. Roughness was the critical difference that saved the stereotype. Then I asked, "Do you mean that the difference in having a lot of fun or just a little fun is in the rough way boys play ball games as opposed to the way girls play ball games?" "Yeah." "Uh-huh!" "Yes, it is." Playing rough meant playing with "more action." It was getting in there and scraping your knees and bruising your chin. It was earning scars to show to your friends. If girls could be rough and tough, as competent as boys in performing "male" tasks—as many of the fourth-grade girls could—what was so special about being a male? If being a good ball player was held up as the male model and there were girls who played as well as boys, then what special kudos were there for being a good ball player? If girls could "hell around"—fight like boys and defy the establishment—what was so great about "helling around?" If girls could share these activities, then the activities were ipso facto devalued. In order to savor the joys of male aggression, violence, and physical conquest, the stereotypes had to remain invulnerable to attack.

Since girls were violating the norms held sacred by boys, how could they redeem themselves in boys' eyes? I asked, "What could a girl do to make you believe she is the kind of person you think a girl should be?" "Well, work around the house, cook, clean the house, not be tomboys, and stop playing boys' games," Chad replied.

At Pine Hill the blatant stereotype of girls' activities did, indeed, serve to persuade girls that they should be in the classroom helping the teacher while the boys played outside. Still, when teacher-imposed game choices demanded that boys include girls on their ball teams, they chose first those—presumably nonexistent—girls who were regulars in kickball or Greek dodge or soccer. Even more telling was the boys' choice of workmates when the teacher insisted that boys and girls share small-group classroom activities; the boys again chose those girls with whom they played ball.

It may be that boys perceived these girls to be more capable academically than other girls and, therefore, a plus to their group project, or perhaps they saw them as less "feminine" than girls who did not play ball and so could permit themselves to share a study project with them without coming too close to the girls' world.

I asked the boys, "If girls enjoy playing ball games, why should they stop playing them?" This question gave the boys an opportunity to express another stereotype, that of the chivalrous gentleman who recognizes the physical weakness of the other sex. "Girls get hurt more than boys," Jonathan explained. The others agreed. "There are two girls on this football team we play on and they even got wiped out of the game by the middle line backer. Man, he goes like this, BOOOMMM! He carries the whole team," said Paul. As men they were expected to protect girls from men like the middle line backer, but how could they when they were in the middle of a game? There was only one solution: exclude girls from boys' games "for their own protection." Then, to prove their good will toward girls, Derek suggested, "Girls should, like, make up different sports for girls and then men wouldn't play them."

To probe the implications of this solution, I asked, "What would happen if the girls made up a game that was very exciting and you really wanted to play it? Would you play it?" Not wanting to turn down a good thing, Jonathan said, "Well, uh, men could play it if it was in a national league or something like that." But what about boys in school? "Suppose the girls at Pine Hill organized a game that was such a great game you really wanted to play it here on your playground. What would you do?" Billy's answer was straight out of the second curriculum: "We'd take over!"

Although I made it a rule to be totally nonjudgmental with the children, Billy's bold assumption that he could simply take what he wanted brought an expression of disbelief to my face. He had spoken with the assurance of one to the manor born; with superior strength and the willingness to use it for personal gain. Derek saw my shocked expression and tried to soften the blow. "It wouldn't matter if boys played the game if it was in school because it wouldn't be a public game," he said. I took advantage of the vulnerability revealed by this. "Do you mean that if boys played a game that was considered a 'girls game' in a place where other people couldn't see you, it would be OK?" "Yeah," he said, and the other boys nodded in agreement. A serious flaw in the second curriculum had surfaced. Their model was for their public, not their private, lives. To a watching world they had to appear "hard," physically strong, skillful on the ball field, scornful of affection and the female world. But here a new dimension, a private self, was showing up.

I was reminded of a conversation I had had with Munro Leaf, the author of *Ferdinand the Bull*. He said that he had wanted to show an autonomous character in that book, a character immune to macho pressures. For this purpose he had chosen a bull, an animal usually characterized as strong, brave, aggressive, and fearless. Ferdinand was everything a little bull should be, but he was also an autonomous individual. While other little bulls butted their horns together and snorted to show how fearless they were, Ferdinand sat under the cork tree and smelled the flowers. He did not have to run with the pack to be happy, as the boys in the Tent Club at Pine Hill apparently did. Munro Leaf said that there had been a Ferdinand in him when he was a young boy. He had done all of the macho things—he was a successful football player both in high school and in college—although he would have preferred to read a book or even write one. Was there also, perhaps, among the Tent Club boys a Ferdinand waiting to be released?

By the end of the fourth grade, the boys' sacredly held stereotypes had been badly shaken by the reality that had been presented to them of girls who played ball as well as most boys and better than some, who ran relay races and won, lifted weights, and competed in high-jump contests and won. It was the girls—the same girls the boys said they did not want in their world—who, in the fifth grade, were to demand equality with boys and get it. But first, the girls had to learn to speak out against the attitudes that had labeled them second-class citizens.

The Pyschological Work of Girls

The psychological work of girls had to do with learning who they were. The early 1970s were marked by a great consciousness-raising movement among women. Women were meeting in so-called rap sessions and learning that the image of themselves they had so faith-fully taken over from men did not actually conform to their own experience of themselves. The girls at Pine Hill were going through a similar consciousness-raising experience. In group discussions I encouraged the girls to express how they felt when boys dismissed them with a stereotyped put-down. The girls had not heard the boys tell me that girls should "work around the house, cook, clean the house, not be tomboys, and stop playing boys' games." They did not have to; they had received that message and many more like it that told them boys did not want them around. They had heard boys laugh at them because the second curriculum had assigned them such despised domestic chores as cooking, cleaning, and sewing. Some girls had fought back, but most had remained silent. Now in our group discussions their indignation was given a serious hearing.

The girls responded to the claim that ball games were for boys only with a counterclaim. "Boys say they like football and baseball and things like that. Well, I know that I do, too. I like football. I like baseball. I like all the boys' sports. It's not fair to say that we don't like them when we do," Angela declared, while the other girls agreed. To the "rough-and-tough" criterion of fun, Sonya conceded that "the boys play rougher than girls and they end up getting hurt," but added, "what's so great about getting hurt if you don't have to?" Socialized by the second curriculum into a world where concern for life was more important than violence to oneself, the girls could not understand what drove the boys to bruise their bodies on the play-ground so that they could acquire scars to prove their manhood. Pain as "fun" was a male, not a female, concept. If the girls who played ball with the boys got to home base on their feet rather than on their knees, as was the custom with the boys, it did not diminish the fun they had had playing the game.

I asked the girls if they knew any girls who were not strong enough to play ball games if that was what they wanted to do, since many, if not all, of the Pine Hill boys were quick to echo first-grader Brian's claim that "girls aren't hardly made for football." Laura conceded that there were some girls who were not made for football. "There are some puny girls. There were a couple of puny girls at the [community] swimming pool. Their names were—oh, I forgot their names—anyway, they were puny." But the label "weakling" did not fit Laura, a champion swimmer. "I got a trophy for swimming. Altogether I got about eight first-place ribbons." She was not "puny"! Nor were any of the girls she knew.

What about puny boys? Had she ever known a puny boy? "Yeah, Jerry Johnson," said Donna. Were there any other boys who were puny? No, she couldn't think of any. By this time the girls understood what I was doing, and Donna said, "Boys say they are the greatest. Well, there are more girls in the world than boys and girls live longer than boys." "Yeah, that's right," said Elizabeth. "And more boys get killed in wars. That's not so great." The other girls agreed.

The girls did not have the problem the boys had of reconciling stereotypes and reality. They were in closer touch with their own reality. They showed an avid interest in discussing their position as related to the boys. They were willing to examine the sex bias in their school books. They were all reading *Caddie Woodlawn*, the true story of an adventurous young tomboy who had grown up on the Western frontier in Civil War days. Caddie had been a frail child, and her father, fearing that she would fall ill and die as her sister Mary had, asked to be allowed to raise Caddie with boys. ". . . I want you to let Caddie run wild with the boys. Don't keep her in the house learning to be a lady. I would rather see her learning to plow than to make samplers, if she can get her health by so doing,"[2] he told his wife, Harriet. Caddie learns to care for the horses and run the farm; when Indians threaten her family and neighbors, it is her courage that saves them. But Caddie's nontraditional socialization brings her life, as she has known it, to a halt when a well-bred female cousin visits from New England and Caddie and her brothers play a trick on her that leaves her in tears. Caddie is punished, sent to bed without her supper, while her brothers do not receive so much as one harsh word. Caddie's father explains why she is the only person to be punished for the prank: she is a girl.

> It's a strange thing, but somehow we expect more of girls than of boys. It is the sisters and wives and mothers, you know, Caddie, who keep the world sweet and beautiful. What a rough world it would be if there were only men and boys in it, doing things in their rough way! A woman's task is to teach them gentleness and courtesy and love and kindness. It's a big task, too, Caddie—harder than cutting trees or building mills or damming rivers. It takes nerve and courage and patience, but good women have those things. A woman's work is

something fine and noble to grow up to, and it is just as important as a man's. But no man could ever do it so well. . . . Do you think you would like growing into that woman now? How about it, Caddie, have we run with the colts long enough?[3]

The girls' first reaction was to the disparity between the punishment Caddie had received and the attitude that "boys will be boys," which exonerated them from culpability. "That's not fair just punishing Caddie when her brothers were in on it, too," Donna said. The other girls agreed. But what about asking Caddie to leave the healthy outdoor life she loved and to stay indoors, an obviously less healthy environment, to sew and cook, while her brothers were not asked to make that choice? "It's not fair to tell Caddie that she can't work with the horses and play outside," said Megan. All of the girls loved horses. They would have liked a horse of their own; they read books about horses from the extensive literature catering to the horse-loving audience of fourth-, fifth-, and sixth-grade girls. Trading a life with horses for an indoor sewing and cleaning job struck the girls as grossly unfair.

Another story had to do with dogs. Late in the school year Laura wrote a book report that compared two blatantly stereotyped animal characters in Dodie Smith's *One Hundred and One Dalmations*.[4] Her report read:

> I am comparing the Red Setter with the Golden Retriever. The Red Setter is a young lady who has not had her puppies yet. She is feather-brained. When something happens she panics. She doesn't have much experience. The Golden Retriever on the other hand is bright, aware, and alert. He works his way out of awkward situations. He is a fine member of dogdom.

With Laura's permission I made a chart of the story and discussed her description of the two animal characters with the whole class, including the boys. We listed their unique characteristics under "He" and "She." From Laura's report the class learned that "She" was (1) feather-brained, (2) inexperienced, which was interpreted by the children to be a pejorative term meaning that she was incapable of being in charge of her own life, (3) easily panicked, and (4) not yet a mother, which was interpreted as meaning that she was essentially useless. On the other hand, "He" was (1) bright, (2) aware, (3) alert, (4) clever, (5) experienced in worldly matters, which was interpreted by the children to mean that he *was* in charge of his own life, (6) resourceful, that is, he worked his way out of awkward situations with ease, and (7) a fine member of dogdom. Since no mention was made of the fact that he was not yet a father, we assumed that his standing in dogdom was not affected, as hers was, by a failure to produce offspring.

There was instant recognition among the children of the bias in favor of males and against females, but the boys smugly assumed that the characteristics were correct. "That's like propaganda," Laura said. "Yeah, that's right! People can't say girls are like that when we're not," Donna declared. The other girls nodded and voiced their agreement.

As yet, there seemed to be little change in the stereotypical attitudes and behavior, especially of the boys, even at the end of the fourth grade. Nor was my success any more notable vis-à-vis their mixed-sex relationships.

The earliest physical contacts between the boys and girls had been in the form of games with few serious emotional elements. Only as the children became older had their contacts acquired more emotional connotations. At this point the lack of an adequate vocabulary to describe the relationships and the accompanying emotions became clear. One of the consequences was a pervasive emotional confusion. "Love," as noted earlier, somehow connoted sex. Even a seven-year-old child knew that. "Love means you want to marry a boy," one little girl told me. She knew because the word had already acquired the giggly aura that went with the underground subject, sex. Even among the fifth-graders, "love" meant marriage and marriage meant sex.

This identification of the word "love" with sexual activity contaminated the word, made it unacceptable except when speaking of mothers and, for girls, teachers and same-sex peers. Sometimes the sexual connotation of the word was felt to be too strong even for family members. "Like" was a more suitable term. Thus fifth-grader Carrie said she liked "only three boys: my dad, Andrew, and Seth [her brothers]." And for opposite-sex peers even "like" was often too strong a word. "What do you mean when you talk about boys liking girls and girls liking boys?" I asked the group. Deprived of any terms for warm, affectionate, friendly relationships between boys and girls that did not imply sexual goals, they were stumped. "In our class," fifth-grader Ramon replied, "It means loving a girl." The poverty of their vocabulary confused them in their attempts to understand how they should behave and feel about opposite-sex peers.

The opposite of "love" was also a problem. Why, I asked a class of fifth-graders, did they avoid the word "love" but use the word "hate" as a substitute for not liking when speaking of opposite-sex peers? Why did they say "don't like" when, as in the case of Dan and Lori, they clearly did like an opposite-sex peer? "Lori really likes Dan but she doesn't want to admit it," Carrie told me and Curtis nodded in agreement. "Dan really likes Lori, too, but he doesn't want to admit it. He brings Red Hots [candy] to school and she goes to his desk and gets them from him." So why couldn't they like one another? What was wrong with a boy liking a girl or a girl liking a boy? Why did they confuse loving and liking, and why couldn't they use the right words to describe how a boy and girl felt about one another? If a boy and a girl wanted to have a "boyfriend-girlfriend" relationship, why couldn't they use the words that would express the special feelings they had for one another?

The boys and girls were ill at ease with these embarrassing questions. They did not know how to answer them. After a long silence Curtis said lamely, "in our class it's just not like that." When prodded further he became annoyed. "I DON'T KNOW! I DIDN'T MAKE THE RULES!"

Carrie was more forthright. "Because you would be embarrassed. Everyone would make fun of you." Boys could say they liked other boys and that was OK. Girls could form best-friend relationships and pledge undying love and no one paid attention. But if a boy and girl said they even liked one another, that was somehow or other wrong.

"If you say you like someone other kids spread it all over the school and that's embarrassing," said Melissa. "If you even sit beside a boy in class other kids say you *like* him. And they come up to you in the bathroom and tease you about liking that boy. Once some of the girls put JS + BB on the bathroom walls. That was embarrassing." "Sometimes kids say things like 'Melissa likes John' when she doesn't even like him and he doesn't like her," added Terese. I turned to John. "How about it, John? Don't you like Melissa?" He looked down at the floor, reluctant to commit himself. "Well, she's OK," he conceded finally. "But I don't like her." "Are you really saying that you don't like Melissa as a friend or that you don't want your name connected with hers as a 'girlfriend'? If you could have girls as friends, would you like Melissa as a friend?" Yes, he would.

Even more painful was the parental hazing the boys and girls were subjected to. Parents shamed and embarrassed their sons and daughters in order to discourage mixed-sex play and, thus, possible sexual contacts. "When are you going to get married?" asked Carrie, parroting in a sing-songy voice her mother's behavior. "I hate that!" she added vehemently. Steven had had a similar experience with his parents. "My mom and dad snicker if they see me with a girl. My mom always looks at my dad and makes faces. That makes me really mad." Other members of the group told similar stories.

Since any kind of affection between opposite-sex peers was presumed to be sexual, it evoked derisive comments or laughter from both peers and adults. To avoid such hazing the boys and girls denied any positive feelings toward opposite-sex peers by claiming to hate them. The hazing, intended to head off sexual relationships, served to make even friendships between boys and girls impossible.

At the end of the first year I was, frankly, disappointed. The year's efforts seemed to have left little imprint. Perhaps, I conceded, I had taken on too big a Goliath. After a year of my confronting stereotypes with reality, the boys were still proclaiming stereotypical attitudes. After a year of my helping them acquire an adequate vocabulary, they still lacked ways to express mixed-sex affection. I consoled myself with the observation that however tenaciously they held on to the stereotypes, they were now defensive about their position and vulnerable, aware that they were open to challenge. At least the girls were protesting the stereotypes vigorously, however unavailing the protests. I was disappointed but not wholly discouraged. Next fall was another school year.

·11·

FADING STEREOTYPES

As had the fourth grade, the fifth grade marked a transition among the boys and girls I was working with, not only in the academic but also in the second, sex-role curriculum. They entered the fifth grade as ten-year-olds who were, it seemed to me, but palpably different from the ones who had left the fourth grade. In the months that separated the end of fourth grade from the beginning of fifth grade, I had not seen the boys and girls. Most of them had spent the summer in the Pine Hill community taking occasional trips to visit grand-parents or vacationing with parents. I had somehow expected that when they returned to school in the fall, we would pick up where we had left off in the spring. As it turned out, however, there seemed to have been an incubative effect in process during the summer hiatus. Seeds had apparently been planted the year before that were now beginning to bud. Only now, in fifth grade, did the boys and girls I was working with begin to talk to one another. But when they did, it proved to be a critical event. They seemed now to be ready to leave the stereotypes behind them and work toward new ways to relate to one another.

I was first alerted to this possibility when Donna, apropos of noth-ing at all, made her statement about marriage. Early in the term, in a voice everyone could hear, she said, "When I'm eighteen I'm going to get married. If the boy I want to marry doesn't ask me to marry him, then I'll ask him to marry me." She had zeroed in on one of the most sensitive issues in the relations between the sexes, the role prescrip-tion that assigned to males the privilege of taking the initiative and to females the onus of waiting. Unabashed, she looked directly at her peers and continued, as though to challenge them, "Why can't a girl ask a boy to marry her?" Jonathan responded, invoking the only sanction he knew. "You can't do that. It's against the law." Aroused to anger by Jonathan's reply, a group of girls challenged him in chorus. "What law?" they asked. Jonathan had to admit he did not know of any such law. He said he had only been teasing. As it turned out, Jonathan, who was one of the most macho boys in the Tent Club but was also the major role transcender of the group, was to play a leading role in the emerging dialogue between the boys and girls in the fifth grade.

It took several seconds for me to grasp the implications of what had just taken place. The kind of dialogue I had been promoting in same-sex groups was now arising spontaneously between opposite-sex peers. I had been urging the girls to challenge the stereotypes whenever the boys parroted them, and now they had taken on Jonathan. I seized the opportunity to keep the nascent dialogue going. "Would you mind if a girl proposed to you?" I asked the boys. "Would it hurt your pride if you didn't have the chance to ask her first?" The girls' eyes were riveted on the boys as they waited for the answer. It was Jeffrey, perhaps the most respected member of the Tent Club, who spoke first. "No, why should it?" This admission from a boy with the reputation of being "cool" made it possible for other boys to join the conversation with the girls as well as with me. Paul asked, "Why should a guy be embarrassed?" Then with a further thought, he added, "especially if he were in high school or college." A proposal to a fifth-grader, he implied, could be embarrassing; he would not yet be prepared to deal with a sexual relationship. But by the time he was old enough—when he was in high school or college—he would be ready for marriage and receptive to such proposals.

Jeffrey explained the boys'—seemingly nonmacho—willingness to let the girls take the initiative in romantic affairs. "Some boys are shy," he said simply. Here was the first pay-off for all of the stereotype challenging we had gone through. Here was reality being recognized. He simply said boys could be shy. Boys could be vulnerable. They had worked hard to fit the stereotypes, to appear cool at all times, and yet here was Jeffrey telling it like it was—that in dealing with girls boys were not always as cool as they pretended to be. They were, in reality, "shy." Laura supported him. "All my life the boys I've known have been shyer than me," she said. As heads nodded agreement, Paul felt compelled to defend the male macho image. "Some girls are shy," he said. "My little sister [aged two] is shy. Whenever someone she doesn't know comes near her, she cries." The children agreed with Paul also. Some girls were shy. But more important than the content of this first dialogue between opposite-sex peers was the fact that it had taken place at all.

Other changes had also taken place between the end of fourth and the beginning of fifth grade. The children were now between ten and eleven years of age and a few of them had reached, or would soon reach, puberty and sexual awakening. They were only two years away from the time when adolescent pregnancy could become a problem for the girls. And, after years of saying that they hated girls and considered them sissies, the boys were now saying that they liked girls. When did this liking begin and what was it they liked about girls?

"We get to like girls at the age of ten and up," Jeffrey said. "We like girls because they are nice, they are pretty, and they are smart. They are different from us boys." Once despised precisely because they were girls, they were now liked precisely because they were girls. The boys liked girls because they had the right qualifications for marriage and motherhood: they were pretty and they were nice. Tommy caught the implication in the message, for he quickly added, "Yeah, and they do all the housework so we don't have to do it." Girls were useful as sex partners, but the boys did not overlook the other important qualification: they were useful for cleaning and cooking and sewing. I was not unaware that there were stereotypes involved here, but there was at least a glimmering of recognition of the incongruity. Jonathan had also caught the message that girls were useful for both sex and housework, but, while he didn't object to either role, he cautioned that girls might object. "Don't say that [about housework]. The girls might get mad." The other boys agreed with Jonathan. They said they should "cool it" on the issue of housework. When the boys and girls had lived in their own separate social worlds, it had not made the slightest difference how girls felt about things boys did and said, but as their worlds began to merge and girls became potential friends, the boys became more considerate of their feelings. The stereotypes were no longer so urgent.

Jeffrey had even added a nonstereotypical attribute to his list of things he liked in girls. He said that he liked girls who were smart. When I asked the other boys, they, too, said, "girls who are smart." When pressed for specifics, they said that they liked girls who "get good grades," "can run fast," "are good ball players," "like to go ice skating at the ice-skating rink," and "have good personalities." At least Pine Hill girls were learning in the mid-seventies that they did not have to play dumb to attract boys.

In the primary grades, however vocal in their dislike of girls, the boys had reluctantly acknowledged that a wife was a necessity and that when they were men and working at a career of their choice, they would have to "get one" to do the cooking, cleaning, baking, sewing, and other household chores that would make their lives comfortable. For they themselves would have nothing to do with such domestic tasks even if they died of hunger or had to go naked. So it was with amazement that I listened to the fifth-grade boys tell the girls that they, too, were eager for marriage and considered eighteen years of age long enough to have to wait for it. Unlike the girls, however, they saw barriers to marriage immediately after high school. Their parents might object because they would want them to get additional training for a job or profession. A boy had to command a salary large enough for a wife and children before he could think of making a marriage commitment. Jeffrey explained: "Boys usually want to get marrried at eighteen. Usually they don't because their parents don't want them to. But they want to. Boys are anxious. Maybe they like a girl a lot and they don't want to wait." There were unmistakable sexual overtones in Jeffrey's statement, but, even so, this was a far cry from "getting a wife" to do the housework. Now the boys were interested in the girls themselves.

What about children? Until now boys had shied away from any association with babies as fervently as they had avoided girls. I asked the boys, "Are you planning to have a lot of children?" Tommy, the oldest in a large family, said, "No, not a lot, but some." He was unable to specify how many "some" might be. Jonathan, however, knew precisely how many children he wanted and he knew what sex he wanted them to be. "I want three," he said. "I hope I'm going to have two boys and a girl. I want the girl to be the oldest so that the boys will respect her. I want the boys to be twins but if it comes out the other way [one boy and twin girls] I don't care."

Jeffrey, the youngest child in a blue-collar family that had to budget its money carefully, was concerned with the expense of raising a family. "I only want one or two children," he said. "I want the boy to be the oldest so he can get a good job and get a good start in life. Boys have to have good jobs so they can support the wife and the kids and the dog and the turtle and the cat." It was a heavy burden a man assumed when he took on the support of a family. The thought of so many mouths to feed prompted Tommy to comment, "That's a lot of young ones. Boy, are you going to have to work hard to support all of those." Jeffrey nodded; his face reflected the seriousness he attached to marriage. "I know it," he answered. But he did not let the stereotype go unchallenged. He would, indeed, have to work hard, very hard, *unless* he married one of the girls in his class who were willing to share the economic burden with their husbands in return for their sharing the work in the home.

How did boys feel about the household chores they were expected to do at home? They said that they did not like doing any kind of household task. Housework, they said, was "boring." Jeffrey admitted that "housework is not too appetizing." "Then who will do the housework when you marry?" I asked. "We will share," they said, meaning that they would share the work in the home with their wives. Then Jonathan, like a seasoned parent, suggested an attractive alternative. "The kids will do it when they are old enough," he said.

Facing the realities of marriage, the boys were coming up with more options than the second curriculum had so far allowed.

There had never been any question about the girls' primary goal even in fifth grade. Marriage and motherhood still loomed large in their minds as the only appropriate career for them. They had also begun to consider working outside the home as an exciting adventure that they wished to experience, but a job was not to take the place of being a wife and mother. Thus Melanie said, "I'd like to get married when I'm eighteen but I'll have a career, too. I might even wait five months [after completing high school] before I get married."

Since marriage still seemed to be the girls' primary career choice, I asked them, "What would you want in a husband?" "That is what I call a good question," said Donna, but before she could supply her answer Elaine said, "Well, that they not be crude and common. You know how boys act sometimes." It was not a question but a statement that both she and the rest of the girls understood: boys could be quite uncivilized in their behavior. When they had food battles in the school cafeteria, for example, and milk cartons, half-eaten sandwiches, catsup, and mustard cluttered the tables and floors and stained the boys' clothing, the girls did not see the antiestablishment value boys found in that behavior; they saw only that boys acted like very young children—like babies, in fact—and they were embarrassed for the boys. The antiestablishment behavior that made boys feel like men made them look like unruly two-year-olds to the girls. They would not want their husbands to shame them with such behavior.

Melanie's next statement opened an area never before explored in the girls' thinking about their relationship with boys. She thought an ideal husband would be one who would "not make us do everything we do." She did not spell out washing, ironing, cooking, and cleaning. She didn't have to. The other girls knew exactly what it was Melanie referred to, and they nodded in agreement. Elizabeth added, "Yes, and not to think we belong in the kitchen." True, it was essential work, but that did not mean ipso facto female work.

Donna criticized the many television commercials she had seen that portrayed an aproned actress beaming over sparkling floors, shining glasses, and shirts with snowy white collars. "I don't believe in that 'Happy Housewife' stuff, do you?" she asked. They had done a variety of housekeeping chores at home and they had never found reason to chortle with joy over any of them. There was nothing pleasurable about staying indoors to wash dishes when they might have been playing out-of-doors with friends. Elaine then made the definitive statement on housework: "It's a lot of pain!"

They had begun by stating what qualities they did not want in a husband: they did not want to marry a man who believed that a woman's place was in the home. But what positive qualities would they want in a husband? It turned out that they had few requirements other than wanting their husbands to be themselves, to work at a job of their choice and to let their wives do the same. Michelle said also that she hoped her husband would be "helpful." When asked if being helpful meant being helpful with work that had to be done in the home, she said yes.

Melanie, still influenced by the second-curriculum model for a successful husband, said, "A boy should be smart." Donna greeted this remark with a display of annoyance. "I don't care about that. A boy doesn't have to be so smart." Laura tried to soften Donna's words. "Well, you wouldn't want him walking around saying, 'Uh! Uh!' all the time would you?" "No boy is that dumb," Donna replied, "I just mean that he doesn't have to be anything special." To be sure of her meaning, I asked, "Do you mean that he doesn't have to be a doctor or a lawyer or have some other important job?" "Yes," she said, "he can be whatever he wants to be. It doesn't have to be anything special." Now that the girls understood Donna's meaning, they, too, agreed that they would not want to marry just for financial security or social status. What they did want was a partnership between equals who shared family responsibilities, work, and play.

On the question of children the girls differed sharply from the boys, who were concerned primarily with the financial costs of child rearing. The girls, by contrast, worried about the day-to-day care children needed. And, as yet, the boys had said nothing that made the girls think they were willing to share that aspect of the marriage-parenthood relationship.

Although the girls continued to consider motherhood a given in marriage, they no longer referred to child care as "fun." All of the girls except Laura, Elizabeth, and Melanie had been assigned child-care responsibilities at home that took hours of time away from their own interests and pursuits. The play-acting they had done in the primary grades had been fun; it had been carried out by peers and rarely lasted more than a half hour. First-grade mothers had had to chase their disobedient children and punish them, but they had not had to pick up their toys, or change their diapers, or feed them, or run after a frisky two-year-old. The real thing was exhausting, and to Elaine—the oldest of four children and a "great help" to her mother—child care, like housework, was a "lot of pain."

Elaine thought that two children would be quite enough for her when she married; Elizabeth and Melanie, although never burdened with child care, said they wanted only one child. Only Laura wanted more than one or two children. "I want an equal number of boys and girls," she said, "so if I get two girls I'll have two more children to get two boys." Donna smiled at her naïveté. "You can't do it that way," she said. Laura sighed. She knew she would take what she got, but it was nice to dream of the ideal family: two boys and two girls.

Laura's plans prompted Elizabeth to comment, "We used to live beside this woman who had thirteen kids." "Gosh, what a lot of pain!" said Elaine sympathetically. "My mom has just four and that's a lot of pain. She can't hardly take care of even four. I do a lot of the work. Those kids are really messy and I have to clean up after them and pick up all their toys." Sensing a sympathetic audience, Donna said, "Elaine and me have everything hard. When I get old enough to have kids they're going to get everything equal. I mean, if I have two kids the oldest is not going to have to do everything for the youngest." Elaine painted an even more descriptive picture of her child-care duties for her eager audience. "I have three kids at home and I do everything for them and then I don't get to go outside and play. I have to set the table and wash the dishes."

Maureen, who was the oldest child in a one-parent, working-mother family, had almost full-time child-care responsibilities after school. I had often seen her trudging home from the supermarket with her arms full of groceries and her younger brother and sister trailing along beside her. She also knew how to make sandwiches and heat soup from a can when they were hungry. "I've been doing everything since I was in first grade. I had to. I was the oldest. My mom, she doesn't sit around and do nothing when she gets home from work, but still I do a lot," Maureen told her friends. Maureen said that she had once suggested that her brother, aged seven, was old enough to contribute his labor to the family, but her mother disagreed. (Three years later Maureen's brother had still not been assigned any household tasks, and Maureen was still complaining about the unequal treatment she felt she had been given.)

The girls sounded a bit like household drudges juggling their time between housework and child care. They were not, of course, but some of them had learned, as Elizabeth noted, that children can be trouble. "Kids are always hanging around causing trouble. They say, 'Mom, can I have a cookie?' 'Mom, can I go out and play?' and then they come in the house with mud on their feet and say, 'Mom, fix me a sandwich.'" Motherhood was definitely not the "fun" they had envisioned in the first grade.

Since twins had been appealingly represented in their textbooks, I asked, "Would you like to have twins?" Jonathan said that he would, but the girls shouted, "NO!" Twins meant double trouble. "I read about this woman who had six babies at one time. She had to heat six bottles. She had to put six babies in the bathtub. She had to wash diapers for six babies," Elizabeth told us. "That's a lot of pain," commented Elaine.

But what if the boys they married wanted twins? For a moment no one answered. Then Donna said, "Yeah, but did you notice that they didn't say anything about wanting to take care of the kids? The boys want us girls to do all the work and we're not going to do it anymore!" The question of child care was already becoming a burning issue with the girls. If the men they married wanted children, how much of their own time were they willing to give to care for them?

With their own experiences to draw upon, the girls began to reassess their career goals. Marriage was still the end result of having been born a girl, but they now thought that there might be other things for them to do. "I'm going to travel and do what I want to do before I get in pain with my children and my husband hanging on me all the time," said Elaine. "Me, too," said Elizabeth. Having fun traveling and doing exciting things were new ideas for these girls. They were beginning to think of themselves, of their own futures outside of the stereotypes.

Other girls had also begun to think of careers outside the home. Donna said that she would like to be either an "architect, secretary, police woman like Angie Dickinson, owner of a donut shop, and/or a teacher." Elaine's choices were, "oceanographer, doctor, paleontologist, or a waitress in a restaurant." Laura said she would like to be an "archeologist, astronomer, or a Spanish teacher." Michelle, who had once thought that she wanted to "clean people's houses," like her mother did, now thought that she would like to be a secretary or a school-bus driver. Donna had written her career choices on a piece of plain white paper, which she decorated with scroll-like lines under which she had written, "CAREER-MARRIAGE-HOUSEWIFE." Although they had not spelled it out as Donna had, the other girls saw their future lives in the same way. First a career for a period of time and then marriage and children.

There were three girls who did not have much, if anything, to say about being housewives and mothers. Regina, Sonya, and Tracey, all good ball players, spent a considerable amount of time in the boys' world as a part of their ball teams. Tracey, it will be recalled, had liked playing ball well enough to change gender identity when she was in the third grade so as to assure her place on the team. When on one occasion she found herself in a group of girls discussing motherhood and marriage, she excused herself from participation and, shrugging her shoulders, said uncomfortably, "I don't belong here. I think I'll go back to class." Later I asked Tracey if she planned to marry and have children when she was grown up. "Well, maybe," she said, as she quickly changed the subject to Little League. "I'm going to play Little League ball this summer. I can hardly wait until school is out." I congratulated her and asked, "When did you first know that you wanted to be a boy?" She replied that she had known she wanted to be a boy at the same time that she knew she wanted to play ball, a boy's game, and got the message that boys did not want girls playing on their teams. The solution: become a boy.

"Starting in kindergarten," she began, "I decided that I really wanted to be a boy. Boys' games are more fun that girls' games. Really there are no girls' games except for playing with dolls, ugh!, or playing hopscotch. Dolls aren't exciting and you don't get any exercise. You just sit around. It's like my sister; she's so fat! She plays with dolls all the time." Tracey paused. She knew she had made an unkind remark about her sister, and she had seen me record it. "Take out that part about my sister," she directed me. "Just say that she's plump. Boy, is she plump." Tracey then continued to explain why she had wanted to be a boy. "When I was littler, we played Greek dodge every day at recess and that is more fun than just sitting around. Every day when we go home we go into this yard and play all these games. Everyone on our street plays. That's fun."

There were adults in the school who worried about the kind of person Tracey would be as an adult. They viewed her as unfeminine and feared that she would never adapt to the female role when the time came for her to be a wife and mother. Tracey's peers were not worried. They liked her. She was regarded as a nice human being, a loyal friend, and a good person to team up with on school projects. When the boys and girls had to choose an editor for the school magazine, they chose Tracey. They were not concerned about her lack of interest in the female world. Tracey had made her choices based on her own unique talents and interests, and she was highly regarded by boys and girls alike. (In ninth grade Tracey was chosen best all-around student, best school athlete, and best-liked student by her peers and teachers.)

"Is Tracey still a boy?" I asked the fifth-grade girls one day, although I knew what their answer would be. I did not, however, anticipate their interpretation of Tracey's behavior. Yes, Tracey was still a boy, but, "We're all boys. And we're girls, too. Do you know what I mean?" asked Donna. I did know what she meant, but I had not known that the girls understood just how androgynous their world had become. This was a giant step for them, and I asked them to clarify what they meant when they said they were both boys and girls. "We're both boys and girls," Donna repeated. "We don't want to be just girls." "Why? What does it mean for a girl to be both a girl and a boy?" "Well, boys get to do a lot of things just because they are boys. Now we are going to do a lot of things, too," Donna replied.

"What kind of things?" I asked. "Well, I'm going to travel and I'm going to have a job," she replied. "Do the other girls feel the same way?" They did. Inside each girl was also a boy waiting for adventure and careers. "I'm going to travel a lot," said Elaine. "I'm going to travel the world over." "Me, too," said the other girls.

In April the children were given their choice of topics for a creative writing assignment. The boys began by saying they were going to write about girls, but they soon abandoned the idea when they found that they were unable to express themselves on paper without feeling "silly." The boys turned to tried-and-true subjects such as scuba diving and Unidentified Flying Objects. Tommy said, "I was going to write about my love life but I don't have a love life so I thought I'd write about the Loch Ness Monster." Tommy had a fairly active love life of hugging and kissing, but he obviously did not mean to reveal this fact publicly. Tommy's sister reported that he had had a change of heart after telling his family that he intended to write a paper on his love life and his father had asked in a voice of impending doom, "What love life?" Such a question might discourage the most determined boy.

The girls, however, experienced no difficulty in writing about boys. They did not write about specific boys and they did not write about their sex games. They wrote about their lives vis-à-vis boys in general.

The All-Age Book With Boys*
By Laura

* How I got this information is: I learned it from my mom and from talking about it with my sister. The part about kindergarten to fifth grade I got because I've gone through those stages.

Well, let's start in kindergarten. I'm ten and it's best starting when you're young. I'm starting this book April 2, 1976. It will be about girls in different stages of their lives with boys. The story ends with becoming a housewife.

Kindergarten
In kindergarten you go through a stage when you start to like boys, but boys don't like you. They run around and call you cooties.

First Grade
In first grade you still like boys and then they sure hate you. And they interfere with your work and you really go down in your work. Boys really hate you until second grade.

Second Grade
In second grade you like boys and they like you. They chase you and try to kiss you but are not serious about it. Then your work kind

of goes up again. You think you're really serious about liking boys, but you're not serious yet. You'll have to wait until fifth grade.

Third Grade

In the third grade you really felt no need for liking boys, but you still liked them, and they still liked you, and that's when their work goes down. You are the age when you really don't get serious but kind of. You do your work most of the time, but sometimes you care for the boys. They call you almost every day, and sometimes you get sick of them when they act dumb. But most of the time they give you tic tacs [candy] and are very nice.

Fourth Grade

In the fourth grade you like the boys and they like you. They do as much to get near you as they can. They sit near you. They do lots of funny things to get your attention. Like making funny noises, hitting you; they keep on bothering you, and they brag in front of you.

Fifth Grade

In the fifth grade you get a little mature and a little serious in liking boys. Then is the time boys start sticking up for you. And they start buying you stuff like candy, a coke, ice cream, lunch, and lots of other stuff.

Sixth Grade

In the sixth grade you are mature and kind of serious about boys. The boys in sixth grade are nice to watch. I guess all boys are nice. The boys in sixth grade take you places and buy you things. But the one thing is they get jealous very easy. So, girls, watch out when you get into sixth grade.

Seventh Grade

In the seventh grade you ARE serious and mature. Boys visit you, and I think all they do is talk. In school they take you to your classes and all over the place. They like to be with you as much as possible. They don't get as jealous as they did in the sixth grade; only a little.

Eighth Grade

In the eighth grade you like the boys and they like you. They are very shy when it comes to girls. They don't know what to do. If you want to talk to them, you would have to be the one to start to talk. And the girls get jealous when they talk to different girls.

Ninth Grade

In ninth grade you like boys and they like you. This is when you get a little shy, and they get over their shyness. That is when they meet you at basketball games or dances, and he is usually with a friend, and most of the time you have a friend with you, too, because you are both very shy at that age.

Tenth Grade

In tenth grade you like boys, and they like you. That's when you start to go on dates alone. You go places like the movies, dinner, lunch, and parties. And you both are not shy at all. And when you get in tenth grade you should not have to stay home and clean house all day. You should have fun but not take things that are bad for you, like drugs.

Eleventh Grade

In the eleventh grade you start to go with boys, and you are just good friends with lots of boys. And the same with boys. You go lots of places with just one boy and sometimes with friends. You see him almost every night, and he tries to be with you as much as he can.

Twelfth Grade

In the twelfth grade you have your boyfriend over for dinner and then to help you with the homework. You go to the ice cream parlor, and he treats. Then you go home to TV downstairs. And you should always have a good time if you have the right date. If you don't have a good time, something is wrong.

College

In college you have to get used to staying away from home. And having roommates. Then you are worried about getting good grades and finding jobs after school. And thinking about when you're going to get married and with whom.

Marriage

When you get married you have to be worried about when and what you are going to fix for dinner and when to clean the house. And you have lots of things to do and to think of. And *you should be sure you're ready to make the big step into a woman.* [Emphasis added]

Housewife

A housewife has to know what she is doing, because you have to clean the house, feed the kids and get them to school, and fix dinner and change the baby, and then feed the hungry DAD. And you married the boy you were once afraid of, and now you have some boys of your own. And you have little girls going through stages like you once were.

The End

The housewife stereotype still lingered on. Although in college you were thinking of finding a job, no job actually shows up in your life as a married woman.

But in the life of the school, stereotypes were failing. Students at Pine Hill were frequently permitted, even encouraged, to take part in the decision-making process in the classroom. In January, the fifth-graders were to elect class officers. Donna, Jeffrey, and Jonathan were nominated by their peers for the office of class president. All three were eager to win, but only Donna and Jeffrey put forth the necessary effort required to win the election. They appointed campaign managers and assistant managers. With the help of these peer-aides the candidates made posters with witty slogans, which they hung on the walls of the school, and buttons of colored construction paper, which were worn by all the children in the school.

For their campaign platforms Donna and Jeffrey chose issues they felt to be of importance to their classmates. Jeffrey chose to be the Law and Order candidate. In his campaign speech he said, "I will focus on a major problem that has been around for a long time: vandalism in our schools. This crime must come to an end. Ms. Bell was recently robbed of her tape recorder and someone took my pen. Just the other day there was a bomb threat at Central High School and a fourteen-year-old boy was found planting a bomb at Richmond Junior High. At Spring Valley Elementary windows were broken and things were stolen. How would you feel if this happened to you? If I am elected I will do my best to keep these things from happening."

Donna chose Truth in Advertising as her campaign issue. In her speech to her classmates she said, "I will focus on one issue, Truth in Advertising. I recently read a true story of false advertising. It is something like this: A girl, eleven-year-old Dawn, came home from school one day and found her sister crying. The reason she was crying was because she had asked her mother to buy her a box of Raisin Bran cereal to get a free record advertised on the back of the box. She wrote for the record and received it but there was no way the record would work. Dawn went to court. This is one of the commercials that uses false advertising: Make Friends with Kool Aid, Kool Aid Makes Friends. If I am elected, I will ask Congress to stop false advertising in T.V. commercials."

A poll of the voters taken by the sixth-graders on Tuesday before the election showed Donna favored to win, with Jeffrey a close second. Jonathan had received only one vote—his own. He had made no attempt to wage a campaign; he had not said one word to persuade his classmates to vote for him. Then, on Thursday, with only two school days left before the election, he came to school carrying bundles of posters under his arms. His little sister trudged behind him with more of the posters he had stayed up all night making. His campaign slogan appeared on all the posters, and as he put them up in the school halls they created quite a stir. They read: "Jonathan Fights for Women's Rights."

In his campaign speech, Jonathan said: "I believe that women should have equal rights with men. If a woman does the same job as a man she should get the same pay. Women should be allowed to get as much education as a man gets. Also, if a woman is good enough to be your boss, she should get the job. How would you feel if someone said you couldn't have a job as a boss just because you're a man? That's not right. So, if I am elected I will see to it that women are treated as equals with men. So, vote for me, Jonathan, because Jonathan fights for women's rights." He won by a landslide vote.

I later asked Jonathan if he had any idea how he had been able to win the election after waiting until two days before voting day to get his campaign going. "I think it was my campaign speech," he said. "People want equal rights for women so I fought for women's rights and won."

It was the following year before I asked Donna why she thought she had lost the fifth-grade election for class president after being ahead of both Jeffrey and Jonathan in the sixth-grade poll. "I think I had a dumb campaign issue. It wasn't something the kids were interested in. The next time I'll pick a better issue like women's rights."

On May 23, 1976, the *Washington Post* reported that the National Organization for Women (NOW) had assigned a task force to examine textbooks used by children in school for evidence of sexism.[1] The newspaper article focused on one story in the Ginn second-grade reader, *The Dog Next Door*, titled, "No, No, Rosina."[2] It was the story of a small girl who lived in the San Francisco Bay area. She and her slightly older brothers were on summer vacation. The boys were permitted to go every day with their father and uncle on their fishing vessel, considered the finest in the fleet. But when Rosina asks if she might be allowed to go fishing too, she learns that girls/women are said to bring bad luck to those who fish in the ocean. Her mama tells her, "Your place is at home." Her brother, Luigi, says, "No, no, Rosina. A fishing boat is no place for a girl." The strongest rejection comes from Papa. "Woman on a fishing boat brings bad luck . . ."

The *Washington Post* article included an account of a visit to a local elementary school to interview second-graders who had read the story. One child, a girl, had "listened carefully and then said that boys had told her that there were things she could not do because she was a girl. 'It wasn't fair not letting her go on the boat,' she said." Then her classmate, this time a boy, was "asked whether it was bad luck for girls to fish. He nodded enthusiastically. 'Yeah,' he said."

The day after the article appeared I read, "No, No, Rosina" to the boys and girls in the fifth grade. I did not mention the story in the *Washington Post* or the fact that this story had been labeled sexist by the National Organization for Women. I wanted to know how they would respond to the content of the story without first having prejudiced them against it. Donna jumped from her chair the second the story ended. She waved her hands in the air to express her indignation. "That's what women's liberation is all about," she shouted. "What do you mean?" I asked. She explained. "Well, her father said that women are bad luck on boats, but she went out on the boat and she didn't bring bad luck; she brought good luck, and that's what Women's Liberation is all about—changing things that people believe about us that aren't true."

"Why do you think Rosina's family believed that women on boats bring bad luck?" I asked. "They never tried it before," yelled Donna and Melanie simultaneously. "They closed their minds to the whole situation. They didn't want to find out whether it was true or not," Melanie added. Then Jonathan asked, "Who wrote that story?" We checked the acknowledgments in the front of the book. The story had been written by a woman. David was surprised; he had not expected to find that the author of a sexist story was a woman. For a moment he was silent as though trying to work out something in his own mind. Then he asked, "When was it written?" The copyright date was 1964. "Maybe that explains it. Maybe she grew up in a place where she wasn't hardly allowed to do anything. If she had been a woman's libber she wouldn't have ended the story like that; only letting Rosina go on the boat one more time. She probably wouldn't have written the story at all," he concluded. David was sure a woman who had been given options in her own life could never have been so sexist in her attitude toward a little girl or another woman.

At that point in the discussion the principal of the school walked into the room with a copy of the *Washington Post* in his hand. "Have you seen this?" he asked. I acknowledged that I had seen the article and had just been discussing "No, No, Rosina" with the children. The principal then told them that a NOW task force had written an analogous story about a black child, a boy, called "No, No, Roosevelt." Roosevelt "wants to go to a white school but is told that if he goes he'll poison the water and everyone will get sick." "It's stupid to believe anything like that," Tommy said. The children had no difficulty understanding the analogy between the black boy, Roosevelt, and the white girl, Rosina; both children had been discriminated against because of a stereotype people held that had no basis in reality. "We've got women's liberation now and things are going to be different," Donna told the principal. He agreed.

As the school year came to an end, the ongoing dialogue between the boys and girls had narrowed the gap between them. Among the boys, Jonathan and Jeffrey had emerged as the strongest advocates for change in sex-role behavior and attitudes, especially those toward girls. Jonathan had won the class presidency on a Women's Rights platform. Among the girls, Laura, Donna, Elizabeth, Elaine, and Maureen had emerged as strong leaders in the movement toward change. The girls had confidence in their ability to bring about change and they had begun to make demands on the boys that would affect their relationships in sixth grade. Elizabeth bought and wore a T-shirt with the legend "The Future is Female." Other girls wrote the feminist slogan "Sisterhood is Powerful" on their notebooks. I certainly could not take credit for all of these changes. A powerful yeast was at work outside the school. Pine Hill boys and girls were not living in a social vacuum.

Changes were also taking place in the school and the community. The PTA held a meeting to examine sexism in parental attitudes and behavior in the classroom. The mother of a fifth-grade girl obtained a real estate license, another returned to college, and another took a refresher course and returned to nursing. Several members of the school staff enrolled in courses in sexism in education. A male teacher read the NOW task force report on sexism in textbooks and stopped using books that appeared in the bibliography. The kindergarten teacher no longer assigned play equipment on the basis of sex. One teacher reported that her mother had returned to school after her last child was out of the house and had earned her master's degree in psychology at the age of fifty-eight.

A great deal had happened to the boys and girls that year. The stereotypes had been confronted and reality faced. But the second objective—the ability to relate to opposite-sex peers as friends rather than as participants in sex games—had not yet been achieved. There was still a year to go, however.

·12·

IT COULD BE DONE

The sixth-graders were now twelve years old. Out of the bits and pieces of the second and third curriculum they were creating a culture of their own, not wholly autonomous because it still had to accommodate itself to adult restrictions, but loose enough to maneuver in. It would be easy to describe the culture of the Pine Hill sixth-graders condescendingly, perhaps from the perspective of an anthropologist or a visitor from a distant planet—a favorite ploy sometimes used to put people down. But the culture the sixth-graders, only months away from their teen-age years, had arrived at was as worthy of respect as any.

Surprisingly androgynous were the peer-group norms of sixth-grade culture, which were revealed when the teacher administered an interest inventory asking what characteristics were most admired in classmates. Once-honored macho traits such as the ability to fight and win, the ability to play ball and win, and the willingness to take on the establishment and win were conspicuously absent from the boys' answers. There was little difference between the answers given by boys and girls. With the harsh macho requirements of the second curriculum out of the way, the boys could admit that they valued friendliness and helpfulness as much as girls did.[1] When the opposite question was asked, "The things I like least in my classmates are. . . ," the answers showed how close the boys and girls were in their attitudes toward same- and opposite-sex peers. The characteristics they disliked—fighting, bragging, unkindness, acting mean, and dishonesty, for example—were the opposite of those they said they valued in friends.

When asked to list their three best friends, the boys and girls disregarded the arbitrary restriction to three and listed all of the friends with whom they spent most of their time, both male and female. For the first time in their elementary school lives, boys included girls' names on their lists and girls included boys' names. Jeffrey said, "I have many friends. Some of them are girls. I really like some of the girls a lot. I really like Melanie a lot. She always seems to

157

be able to get all of her work done in school and never has to take it home. But I just like friendly people and it doesn't matter whether they are boys or girls." With such strong peer support behind their actions, both boys and girls became able to maintain girl-friend and boy-friend relationships openly. Such friendships could come out of the closet.

Going Steady

Having friends of the opposite sex did not discourage the children's interest in sex games, but it did pose new problems for them. How were they to distinguish between a girl-friend–boy-friend and a "going-steady" (girlfriend-boyfriend) relationship? Without any conscious effort on their part to establish guidelines for the girlfriend-boyfriend relationship, certain characterizing practices came to be observed. Among these girlfriend-boyfriend practices were: (1) congregating weekly at local "hangouts" with other "steadies" in the group, (2) making nightly phone calls to girlfriends and boyfriends, (3) exchanging gifts on birthdays and holidays, and (4) being responsive to one another's feelings in matters that affected the relationship.

The Hangout

There had to be somewhere outside of school where friends could meet and continue their contacts. The neighborhood shopping center served this purpose for the Pine Hill sixth-graders, who made arrangements to go there in groups. Often they just walked around and looked at things in store windows and talked with other friends they met there. Sometimes they shared a pizza, ice skated, bowled, or went to a movie. What they did depended upon the amount of money they collectively had, but the activity was less important than the fact of meeting in the prearranged way, which they defined as dating. The location of the shopping center—it was within walking distance of the Pine Hill community—was considered a safe place for boys and girls their age. Merchants knew them and their families, often on a first-name basis. The boys and girls who lived farthest from the school and the shopping center were taken home by the parents of those who lived within walking distance. They were more protected than were older boys and girls who frequented the same hangout.

The Nightly Phone Call in Sixth-Grade Culture

On weekdays, when schoolwork and an early curfew kept the boys and girls in their homes after dinner, the phone was their one vital link to their peer world, and they used it as frequently and as long as they could. The phone achieved an almost ritualistic importance in their lives, and only parental wrath could keep them from fulfilling this obligation to steadies. Although the children saw one another for eight hours and more during the day, it was on the phone that they made plans for group dates, argued and "broke up," exchanged information about homework, and discussed their relationships with other peers in their class. They did not regard these conversations as private, that is, between only two people, for any communication that took place at night was sure to be repeated the following day at school. In this way the entire group brought pressures to bear on one another to maintain appropriate standards of behavior between girlfriends and boyfriends.

There was another kind of phone call girlfriends and boyfriends made to one another—the anonymous phone call—which gave them the sense of taking part in a spy thriller. Thus, on one occasion Elizabeth told her friends at school that her boyfriend, Jeffrey, had phoned her the previous night and said, "This is the humane society. You will have to keep your dog tied up." Then he hung up. "I waited for a few minutes and then I called him back and said, 'This is the zoo. Twenty of our elephants got out and one is still missing.' Then I hung up. He still doesn't get it," she said, as she fell laughing onto Melanie's shoulder. During the school day this story was told and retold many times. Only then did Jeffrey finally realize that he was the missing elephant and that the joke was on him.

The Gift Exchange

The exchange of gifts on birthdays, Christmas, and Valentine's Day in the sixth-grade culture was as important to maintaining the illusion of an adult dating relationship as were the weekly trips to their hangout and the nightly phone calls. Christmas presented a unique situation, for almost all of the boys and girls were going steady and all were thinking about the gifts they would give and receive. They discussed these gifts in same-sex groups, and, perhaps to avoid invidious comparisons, the girls as a group decided to give the boys posters for their bedrooms, and the boys settled upon birthstone rings for the girls. It was this gift exchange that alerted parents not already aware of the going-steady arrangements that their children had girlfriends or boyfriends. Jonathan's mother, for example, said that she realized that Jonathan spent a whole lot of time phoning Laura at night, but she had not realized that they were going steady until he bought her the birthstone and came home with the poster she had given him. She remarked that "children are growing up too fast these days."

Birthdays were occasions for the expression of individual tastes and interests. Thus, on Tracey's birthday Tommy gave her a ballpoint pen that had been advertised on television so frequently that everyone in the class wanted to own one. He had wrapped the gift in a brown paper bag, tied it with string and presented it to her at school, where all their peers could see what he had given her. The gift was an instant success with both Tracey and the other girls. Paul gazed at it in admiration and said, "That's a great pen. I sure wish I had one." The relationship between Tommy and Tracey was the only boyfriend and girlfriend relationship to remain intact throughout the entire school year.

Valentine's Day was almost as important to the students of Pine Hill as Christmas. The entire school took on an aura of excited anticipation as large envelopes made of red construction paper were hung on each child's desk to hold the many cards they hoped to receive from friends. In the sixth grade a new dimension was added to the Valentine card exchange, for the boys and girls decided to spend their allowances buying small gifts for steadies. The Valentine gift was as important to maintaining group norms and cohesiveness as it was to the relationships between the boys and girls. Possibly more so.

Changing Attitudes

Up to this point in elementary school, second-curriculum rules for the girlfriend and boyfriend relationships had specified that they be kept secret. In the sixth grade they were brought out into the open. The boys and girls invited one another into their homes. They discussed their interest in one another with parents. They did not define boyfriend and girlfriend relationships as implicitly sexual. Once they understood this new kind of relationship themselves, they could explain it to others. The going-steady relationship was flexible enough to permit exchange of partners several times during the school year, and because it was a group, rather than an individual, affair they could change girlfriends and boyfriends with no loss of continuity in their social group.

The going-steady relationship was so nonthreatening that it could even intrude into the traditionally same-sex slumber party, as it did on one occasion with pleasant results for all. Elizabeth had invited the girls in the class to a slumber party to celebrate her birthday. The boys could not have expected to be invited to a slumber party, but they did not take their exclusion lightly. They found a way to attend. Jonathan, representing all the boys, phoned Elizabeth's mother and asked if they might surprise the girls by arriving at eight o'clock to join the party. They promised to leave at eleven, when they would go to Jonathan's house to spend the night. With her permission, they arrived armed with potato chips and soft drinks. They danced and talked with the girls until Jonathan's mother arrived to take them home with her. Elizabeth's grandmother, visiting from another state, was surprised at this turn of events and remarked, "Those boys and girls really seem to like one another. Nothing like this ever happened when I was a girl."

Instead of fearing them, some of the mothers came to see the benefits of opposite-sex friendships and could even welcome steadies into their homes. Tracey, for example, became a frequent visitor in Tommy's home, sometimes staying for dinner with his family. Equally often, he visited in her home. "Does your family approve of your going steady with Tracey?" the sixth-graders asked Tommy. Before he could answer, Jeffrey asked the other burning question, "Do they even know you're going together?" Yes, they knew.

Fathers were not always so supportive. Not even as sixth-graders were the boys completely spared the hazing about sex that they had endured in earlier grades, especially from fathers and mothers. It was still assumed that boy-girl relations had to be intrinsically based on sex. Tommy's younger brother teased him, but his father was "worst of all. He wants to know when I'm going to get married. I hate that!" Jonathan concurred: "Yeah. All dads are bad that way. They say that you really have to know how to make it with a girl and that we're too young for that. I hate it when they say things like that." Such harassment, however, no longer had the sting it once had. The boys were becoming comfortable enough with the subject of sex that they were not intimidated by the suggestion that male-female relationships had to be sexual. Peer support provided the security they needed to make the decision to be a girl-friend or a boy-friend rather than a girlfriend or boyfriend.

"Breaking Up" and "Making Up"

Going-steady arrangements were never long-term—with the exception of Tracey and Tommy—and frequent arguments resulted in "breaking up." Two days before Valentine's Day, for example, Paul purchased a large chocolate kiss wrapped in silver foil to give to Megan. But they broke up and he consoled himself by eating the candy himself. The next day at school they "made up," but he had no gift to give her the following day, Valentine's Day. Nor did he have the money to buy one. A cash advance from his mother on his babysitting job saved the day for Paul.

The use of the terms "breaking up" and "making up" were a part of the constant attempt by the boys and girls to be as adultlike in their peer relationships as possible. What older siblings did, they did. Like adults, they insisted that the opposite-sex peer who was their current steady was their only true love and that this relationship was destined to last forever and ever. When on one occasion I suggested to Donna that her romance with Derek was not true love and that she would have many boyfriends before she married, she replied angrily, "Oh, yeah! Well, that's all you know! This is forever!" But it was only a short time later when she and Derek quarrelled and broke up.

Donna's break-up with Derek happened at the same time that Elaine broke up with Chad, and although the two girls discussed their grievances against the boys with one another, they were angry when they found the two boys doing the same thing. They had come upon the boys huddled together in the classroom after lunch when the other students were outside on the playground. As they walked through the door they heard their names being spoken. When they asked the boys what they had said about them, the boys would not answer. Their refusal infuriated Donna, and when the others returned to the classroom she told them, "One thing I don't like is to walk into a room and find them [the boys] talking about us. Boys always talk about girls and this is one thing I don't like about them. Some people say that girls talk about boys all the time. Well, we don't ask our girlfriends every little thing we should say or do to the boys. When Derek wants to say something to me he runs to some other boy and asks if he should say it! He says, 'Should I say this to Donna?' What a weirdo! I don't run to my girlfriends to ask if I should say something to Derek. I know what is going to happen tonight. The last time we broke up he called me at home and made me feel sorry for him so I took him back. When he calls me tonight I'm going to say, 'I never want to see you again!' Then I'm going to hang up!"

Donna was less angry about her broken heart than about Derek's refusal to tell her what he had been saying about her. It was a dramatic moment and the boys and girls took it seriously, although Donna would have been hard pressed to explain how she would manage never to see Derek again when they shared the same classroom and the same friends. Jonathan expressed skepticism. "Oh, yeah! I'll bet you'll take him back when he calls tonight. He'll tell you he's sorry and you'll feel sorry for him and tomorrow you'll be going steady again." Jonathan was right. The next day they were going steady again. A short time later, however, Donna and Elaine exchanged boyfriends. The switch in steadies did not affect their relationships with ex-steadies or the composition of their social group.

In addition to these practices, there were also certain rights implicit in opposite-sex relationships.

The Right to Demand Change

The boys had never taken as much care about their appearance as girls had. They appreciated the way the girls had their hair cut and the neat, attractive way they looked, but they did not think they themselves had to be particularly careful about their own appearance. When they were in fifth grade the girls had begun to resent the emphasis on their appearance and the boys' neglect of their own. At that time Donna had expressed how the girls felt about the situation. "The boys want us to be pretty. How about their being cute? They never care about hurting our feelings telling us we *have* to be pretty. Now we're going to hurt them back." Melanie agreed. "That's right," she said. "Boys don't care what a girl *is* as long as she's pretty. She can be real mean but if she's pretty they don't even notice. But mostly they just don't care about anything else about a girl." "Well, if we have to be pretty, then they'd better start being cute," said Elizabeth. But that was in the fifth grade, and the girls were not yet making such demands directly to boys. In the sixth grade, they were.

The entire class had gone to an outdoor camp for a week under the supervision of their teachers and other adults. On the first day they had hiked up the hill to get to their cabin and then gone through a series of activities that included learning to climb a large, tall tree, walking on logs, preparing their lunch, and cleaning the cabins. That night the girls showered, washed their hair, and put on fresh clothing for a special event that was to take place around a campfire. The boys arrived wearing their soiled clothing and smelling, the girls said, like "dead rats" and "decaying fish." The girls angrily told the boys that they considered their appearance a personal insult and that they would have nothing to do with them until they cleaned themselves up. Then they put as much physical distance as they could between themselves and the boys. The next day the boys appeared showered and in clean clothes. They had apparently decided that cleanliness and a neat appearance were better than ostracism by the girls.

Friendship and Love

Now that the boys and girls had had the opportunity to experience two kinds of relationships with opposite-sex peers—one based on physical attraction alone and the other on mutual liking and interests—they could evaluate them and decide what the differences were between them, if any. On one occasion group consensus was with Donna, when she said, "Sometimes you have a better relationship with a person of the opposite sex when you are not a girlfriend or a boyfriend. When you are just friends you can get along better." She was referring to the fewer pressures placed on friendships. Being a girlfriend or boyfriend meant being at someone's beck and call. They found this confining, for it meant, on occasion, having to sacrifice one's own plans to fit into another person's schedule.

There was also the "chicken and egg" problem: did friendship lead to love or love to friendship? Laura, whose habit it was to explain things to herself by writing down her thoughts, concluded that friendship was the necessary first step in any relationship with an opposite-sex peer. Then as the boy and girl got to know and like one another, they would also care for one another. Caring, said Laura, was loving. This is how she stated her case:

Friendship into Love

Friendship will slowly bring you to love. When that happens it will not be puppy love and it will not be plain love, but it will be young love. Young love may be difficult for some people to understand because they think we are very young. But even if you are young, if you try hard to know someone better you will slowly feel close to that person. Then when you are both older and more mature you will be able to care for one another.

There are some people who will not understand how it is possible to have a friend of the opposite sex. They feel that boys and girls cannot relate to one another because they are not the same sex. These people feel weird and strange when a person of the opposite sex is around. For example, when I was younger I liked a certain boy in my neighborhood but when he came to my house I felt weird around him. I felt strange. I felt as though I did not know him at all, as if I had just met him. But I don't feel that way now about the boy in my class I like now. When he comes to my house I try to make him feel at home. I don't feel weird around him because even though he is my boyfriend he is also my friend and I like him.

Of course there are some things boys can't share with girls and some things girls can't share with boys. Obviously you can talk with friends of your own sex about personal things like your body but you can't talk with opposite-sex friends about those things.

Young love and friendship are funny things. When boys and girls are around eleven years old it is easy for them to be friends. When they are fourteen or fifteen they are shy with one another and then it is not so easy. I know that because my brother and sister are those ages and they are shy with opposite-sex friends.

The freedom to form friendships with opposite-sex peers was giving the boys and girls the opportunity to explore one another's minds and emotions rather than one another's bodies in the tool shed or darkened hallways of an apartment building. They were pleased with this new friendship relationship.

Three years later, when they were in ninth grade, they were to tell a television reporter that this network of friends—both same- and opposite-sex peers—had provided them with protection from adolescent pressures to prove themselves sexually. They said, also, that being able to use words to express feelings about love, sex, and friendship had been another kind of protection. "We're not embarrassed to talk about love and sex because we talked about these things a lot in elementary school and we know we're not mature enough at our age for a real love relationship."

So much, then, for friendship in the culture of sixth-graders at Pine Hill in the late 1970s.

The Future

My four years with this one class of boys and girls were coming to a close. I was curious to see what they were thinking now that they were about to leave Pine Hill. I asked them what their hopes were for the future. What did they want their world to be like? Here is what three of them said.

Laura:
The future is helping one another to become whatever is right for them. It should be whatever a person wants it to be and not what someone else thinks it ought to be. A person should be able to decide where he or she wants to live and how. A person should be able to get married or stay unmarried if that is what he or she wants.

People my age change their minds a lot because we get different ideas as we grow older so I can't really say what I want to be. Sometimes I think I would like to be an actress and at other times I think I would like to be an astronomer and study the stars. But it is hard to choose a job when you don't know anything about it so I would like to learn more about all kinds of jobs so that when I go to college I will really know what it is I want to be. It is good to think about the future when you are young because it helps you to make the right decisions about your life when you are an adult.

Jonathan:
In the future I believe that job relationships will not be as important to men as personal relationships. Men will spend more time with their families. I think that eventually the Equal Rights Amendment will be passed and then women will be considered equal with men. Since young women mature faster than men and have higher scores

on tests I think that in the future the scale will begin to tip towards the female side. Very soon we may have our first woman president.

Eventually there will be more women in non-contact sports because they have more stamina than most boys. For example, in my elementary school we had an Olympics. In the high jump a girl beat all the boys and went for the record. Women will not be better than men in contact sports such as football, boxing, and wrestling because men have stronger arms for throwing and stronger legs for running.

More women will be in the armed services. For a long time women have been W.A.C.S., W.A.V.E.S., and even generals. I doubt that women will ever be in the fighting units such as infantry and tank units. They could man jets and fighter planes just as well as men.

But, no one really knows what the future holds for people. We will just have to wait and see.

Elaine:

Today in the business world women have a lot more chances to get the jobs they want for their careers. Just a few years ago such jobs as policemen, plumbers, firemen, truckers, and football players were for men only. Now women are allowed to do these jobs, too. Women can be what they want to be. There was a time when women could only choose from a category of boring jobs such as: sewing machine operator, secretary, teacher or nurse. Today women want jobs that are more challenging. They want to do things that they enjoy and that are exciting.

Today, if a woman wants to be a construction worker she can be one. If a man wants to be a seamstress, he can be one. Men and women get paid the same when they do the same job. They get the same benefits. They get the same opportunities on the job. Now that's EQUALITY!

Not, I thought, a bad prospect for the future.

While what boys and girls wrote on an assignment was interesting, it could mean only that the sixth-grade culture had assimilated the words. Had our four years together really made a difference? Was it possible to succeed against the traditional modes of socialization? Since my four-year association with the Pine Hill boys and girls had not been intended as a formal research enterprise or as a demonstration project, I had not planned to measure the results achieved at the end of the sixth grade. I could not answer these questions.

As it turned out, however, validation of the changes did occur, almost adventitiously, by way of a television show on a local news program. It so happened that the day the television reporter scheduled her visit to the school was the day of the annual special sports events. It was the first time that boys and girls at Pine Hill had ever competed with one another in the same events. Compliance with Title IX[2] conflicted with tradition, and only this one group of Pine

Hill boys and girls had agreed to integrate the sports events. Throughout the rest of the school students continued to compete in same-sex groups.

When it was over we all sat with the television interviewer to discuss with her what had happened. Both the boys and girls admitted that they had been somewhat uneasy when they had first thought of competing against one another in this all-school event. "We thought the boys would beat us in a lot of things," admitted Donna, and Chad provoked general laughter when he echoed her comment: "And we thought the girls would beat us in a lot of things." They were both right. Boys did beat girls in a lot of events; girls did beat boys in a lot of others. But not always in the expected way. As it happened, Paul won the jump-rope prize; Laura won in the 60-yard dash and the standing broad jump and was second in the high jump; Tracey won the high jump at a record of three feet ten. Title IX had proved feasible and acceptable. But it had done even more.

Although in the course of the discussion there was talk about winning, it now no longer appeared to be a life-or-death matter to the boys. It was no longer essential for group acceptance, nor did losing mean rejection by peers. Derek was able to say, "I don't have to win. It's just fun to play the game." With winning and losing no longer a life-or-death matter, boys could admit girls even into the competitive races, both in sports and in the classroom. But losing to a girl? Wasn't that different from losing to a boy? "What do you think of the idea of a girl's beating you?" the television interviewer asked. "Well," was Paul's reply, "you just have to try to get better." If you wanted to win and didn't, then you had to practice to improve your skills.

So far from fearing competition with girls, the boys welcomed it; it made the game more fun. Why? Because it increased the number of available players. "Before we always played against the same kids, the boys, and it's more fun when more kids compete." "Some of the girls are better than the boys," Paul assured the reporter. Derek agreed that the girls they played with were good. "Yeah, some of the girls are lots better." There was Laura to prove his point. "It's like when we were lifting weights one time, Laura beat me at weight lifting." Chad also had a good word for the girls, especially Tracey. "She's on our soccer team and she's better than a lot of the boys on the team."

The boys were eager to disabuse the interviewer and the television audience of any traditional views they might have held about the caliber of the girls they played with. Like the girls, they could therefore envision equality between the sexes in sports, in the home, and in the marketplace. Of course, the girls they played with were a select group; they did not play with sissies. These were girls worthy of the boys' mettle.

The interviewer asked how they had changed since third grade. "We're lots different," replied Derek. To the reporter's "How?" Chad answered, "In the third grade we didn't want to play with girls. We thought anything girls did was sissy stuff but now we know better." And Paul, remembering the days when the boys had chased girls from their games and told them to make up their own games and leave boys' games alone, added, "We used to fight with them a lot."

The reporter asked me if I thought it had been difficult for them to give up their macho attitudes and the constant striving to prove themselves. Yes, I thought it had. It had taken a lot of psychological work for them to replace stereotypes with reality. It had called for a lot of reinforcement and encouragement for them to reach a point where they could look into a television camera and tell parents, teachers, siblings, younger children in the school, the community, and the world at large that they no longer accepted the stereotypes about girls. They were able to say that having—skilled—girls to compete with added to the fun.

The girls came to the question "How did you feel about playing against the boys?" from a different angle. "I don't think about it that way," said Laura, who had beaten the boys in a number of events that day. "We're all friends whether we are girls or boys and it doesn't matter who you play against as long as you're having fun." In winning she had not put anyone else down; she had simply demonstrated her own skill. Tracey agreed with her. "I don't think it matters if boys and girls compete because they are your friends and it is fun to compete with your friends. It doesn't matter who wins. Why should only boys compete with boys and girls with girls? It's the same; it doesn't make any difference."

But perhaps all these changes would have occurred anyway? The times were auspicious for change. The women's movement had produced a new orientation. Perhaps I had had nothing to do with the elimination of stereotypical sexist attitudes, with this egalitarianism they expounded. I had no way of proving it one way or the other, but the attitudes and behavior of these sixth-grade boys and girls contrasted sharply with the attitudes and behavior of the other children who were still playing among themselves in the nonintegrated sports events. The camera highlighted the traditional same-sex groupings in all these activities. The children participating in them had not been subjected to three years of persistent change, they had not been exposed to the contrast between stereotypes and the reality around them, they had not had to revamp the third curriculum to include friendship between opposite-sex peers.

Whatever my own contribution may have been, I felt a considerable amount of satisfaction in the knowledge that the battle against stereotypical sex roles was winnable. It wasn't easy. But it was possible. It could be done.

But did the changes last? Could they withstand the pressures to conform in junior high school? I kept in touch with them for several years as they moved through junior and into senior high school. The changes lasted at least that long. Whether they could survive the backlash of the 1980s I do not know. I have no proof. All I have is hope.

EPILOGUE

One of the main objectives I had had in mind for the Pine Hill boys and girls had been to free them from the gender-role stereotypes that were having such limiting effects not only on their academic aspirations but also on their interpersonal relations. The evidence presented here seemed to show that the objective had been achieved at the time they left elementary school. But would the results last? In the sheltered environment of Pine Hill it had been relatively easy to disregard the gender stereotypes. But how about the peer pressures in junior high? Could these boys and girls continue in their new pattern?

I did not know. No funds were available for follow-up, but group interviews made for television[1] supplied some of the answers. The first was discouraging; the second, reassuring.

The First Interview: Seventh Grade

On one occasion, when Laura called Chad a "nice boy" because he did not make suggestive remarks to girls or judge them solely on the basis of their physical charms, her approving remark—and Chad's smiling response—rendered him suspect in the junior-high crowd. He became the butt of their jokes. How, his new peers asked, could a boy be a real man if he did not "take his sex when and where he could get it?" Under these pressures he had broken. He strove manfully to blot out his image as a "nice boy," to build a macho reputation, even it it involved repudiating his long-time friendship with Donna. Thus if she approached him when he stood talking with male peers he ignored her. In this new environment it was forbidden to be her friend and at the same time maintain any kind of relationship with his recently acquired male friends. Score one for the peer group.

In the case of the girls the culture of the new peer group was less punitive but equally seductive. Laura, Donna, Elaine, and Maureen became pom-pom girls; they said they went to school to see the boys. When asked by the television interviewer if boys were all that important to them, Donna exclaimed, "That's all there is right now! We go to school so we can see the boys. We walk down the halls with our

170

girlfriends and say, 'Look! Look at that neat guy!' It gives us something to look forward to each day." Except for Tracey and Elizabeth the girls were attracted to the glamorous and even "sexy" professions. They talked about becoming models and airline attendants when they grew up. Score 2 for the peer group. I felt their Pine Hill experience had not achieved very much. Still, they did express the hope that I was not too disappointed with them.

The maintenance of friendships with opposite-sex peers was difficult in this new school setting. In the predominant peer culture the old stereotyped notion that relationships between the sexes should be limited to love—that is, sex—was once again a reality to be dealt with. Thus, in the first TV interview in junior high school, Jonathan told the reporter that he felt uncomfortable about sitting beside a girl in the cafeteria because she immediately assumed that he wanted to date her. Other boys said that they felt uneasy about even starting a conversation with a girl since this gesture of friendship would, no doubt, be misconstrued as romantic interest. The girls felt the same constraints in approaching opposite-sex peers. The case for the girls was bluntly stated by Laura. "In this school boys either like you for your body or they don't like you at all. When I walk down the hall boys say, 'You're too flat. I'm not going out with you.'"

The night this interview was aired the phone at Laura's house rang incessantly. She received one harassing phone call after another. Other girls wanted to know why Laura would alert parents and other adults to the kind of interplay that went on between opposite-sex peers at the junior high school. How could she hope to be popular with boys if she talked so openly about what they said and did? Only the strong position of her brother in the school saved her from further persecution. She had learned that her new peers expected girls (and boys) to keep their relationships with opposite-sex peers secret.

From Jonathan's mother I learned how powerful—even punitive— male peer pressures could be when the boys called him "queer," "fag," and "gay" because of his poor performance in sports resulting from the camping accident that had deprived him of his skill. The intensity of the suffering inflicted by the taunts showed up when she found him in his bedroom one evening staring at a knife in his hands, questioning the worth of life. Fortunately he learned to perform daredevil stunts of skill that did not involve the use of his feet.

After this interview I felt pessimistic. But an interview with a NOVA producer when the boys and girls were in ninth grade revived my spirits.

The Second Interview: Grade 9

Gender Labeling of Courses

The interviewer wanted to know if the ninth-graders had encountered any gender-labeling of academic courses. "Do you feel that there are some courses you should or should not take because you are a boy or a girl?" she asked. "Some people say that 'this is a girl's course so boys shouldn't take it' but I don't think we should be so limited. Boys and girls should be able to take any course they want. If a girl is interested in auto mechanics and wants to take that she should be able to take it and if a boy wants to take gourmet cooking he should be able to take it," said Jeffrey. "And," said Elizabeth, "if a girl doesn't want to take cooking she shouldn't feel she has to take it. I wouldn't want to take any kind of cooking class because I hate to cook. When I get married I'll serve TV Dinners to my family. I don't care what I eat as long as I don't have to cook it. What I'd really like is a husband who will do the cooking but most guys don't want to do that."

Careers

"Do you think of what you will do when you get out of school in terms of what will be available or in terms of your own interests?" asked the interviewer. "You have to think of what will be available," said Jonathan. "I would like to be a lawyer but a lot of people won't hire young lawyers. Your grades have to be really good to even get into a law firm." "We took a course on careers," said Megan, "and the people who talked to us said that there will be a demand for architects in the 1980s so I thought that might be a good career for me." "When we get out of high school everything is going to be electronic," said the scientific-minded Elizabeth. "This is the space age, you know, and we'll all have to be computer scientists. Just going to college isn't going to be enough education. We'll have to go to graduate school or into an apprenticeship program."

Paul admitted that the discussion about careers and the future frightened him. "Having to be an adult kinda scares me. I don't know what kind of future I'm going to have but I know that I have to get serious about school so that I can get a good job someday. I'm not looking forward to what's ahead. Sometimes I wish I could go back to being a little kid in elementary school. I wonder what it will feel like to be an adult." "What do you think it will feel like?" asked the interviewer. "I don't know," Paul replied. "I don't know either," admitted Jonathan, "but I think that it will be hard. There will be fewer job opportunities and everyone will be trying to get the same jobs."

Marriage

"Do you think there are more pressures on boys than on girls because boys are going to be the husbands and fathers and will have to bring home the money they earn to take care of their families?" asked the interviewer. "No," said the boys, "there are more pressures on girls." "Why?" asked the astonished interviewer. "Because," replied the boys, "the girls are going to be wives and mothers *and* have jobs."

"Do all of you feel that girls have more pressures on them than boys?" asked the interviewer. "Yes," said the girls. "We want to get married and have children but we want careers, too," explained Elizabeth. "The guys really don't have to take care of the kids. If you look around you it is the mothers who are doing things for their kids, not dads. It's not that mothers care more, but they do more." "The problem is," explained Elaine, "boys think it isn't macho to be around little kids."

Sports

Sports was another area the interviewer probed to find evidence of sexist attitudes. "You must be really good at sports, Tracey," the interviewer said. "Are you on the sports team?" Tracey replied with a brief, shy "yes," but her peers lavishly praised her as the best sportsperson among them. "Tracey will be a star soccer player some day," said Jonathan. "She's really good," agreed Chad. "She plays basketball and wins every game." "Basketball on the girls' team or the boys' team?" asked the interviewer. "On the girls' team. The boys have their own team," Tracey replied. "Don't you have integrated sports at your school?" asked the interviewer. "Track," they replied. "Are you on the track team, Tracey?" the interviewer asked. "Yes," Tracey replied, "but when our team plays against other teams they won't let me play." "Why not?" asked the interviewer. Jonathan explained. "Our teachers say that girls are fragile and boys might hurt them if they play in the same game. But the real reason is that in junior high school they [teachers] do everything by sex."

Games

Noting the puzzled expression on the interviewer's face, Donna tried to explain. "When we were younger our teachers let us play together but now that we're older teachers don't want boys and girls playing together because they think there will be physical contact." "And adults don't like it when there is physical contact between boys and girls?" asked the interviewer. "That's right," said Jeffrey. "Our teachers let us play football together but games where we touch one another's bodies give them problems." "Do you think this is an adult problem they are putting on you?" asked the interviewer. "It's their problem," said Jonathan. "Games where boys and girls have to touch gives adults problems." "That's true," said Elaine. "Teachers think it is terrible if a boy and girl touch one another. They think the girl will get a big [pregnant] stomach from that."[2]

Dating

The interviewer wanted to know about the dating customs of teen-agers. "Can girls phone boys and talk to them as friends or do girls wait for their boyfriends to call them?" she asked. "We should be able to phone boys and talk to them as friends but some kids in our school don't understand that," said Donna. "The other day when I was at home I phoned a boy I know and a girl who was with me said, 'Girls aren't supposed to call boys on the phone.' That's a stupid way to think but there are a lot of kids who think that way."

Megan said that she had had similar experiences. "I just can't get some of my friends to understand that when I call a boy on the phone it is because we are good friends." "Why do you think your friends feel a girl should not call a boy on the phone?" asked the interviewer. "They think we're being too pushy," said Elaine. "And they think that boys won't like it if girls are pushy?" asked the interviewer. "That's right," said the girls.

"When does dating start and what does dating mean?" asked the interviewer. "Right now it doesn't mean anything," said Maureen matter-of-factly. Jonathan explained. "Guys meet girls they like at the shopping center or the mall but it's not really a date. When a guy likes a girl and asks her to go with him that means she will meet him somewhere like at the skating rink. On Friday night everyone goes to the skating rink to meet their girlfriend or boyfriend. The seniors call it 'mass dating.'"

"Are there pressures on you to be dating? Do people say you should or should not date?" asked the interviewer. "None of the guys drive so we don't have real dates," said Donna. "I don't know what my dad would say about a car date. He doesn't mind if a guy calls me on the phone and asks me to meet him somewhere but I think he'd be upset if I went out in a car with a guy." "Do you think your parents are concerned that you might have a sexual relationship with a boy if you went on a car date with him?" asked the interviewer. "Is that why they are so afraid?" "I guess so," said Donna. Elaine replied with absolute certainty, "Yes, that's it!"

Although research shows that the influence of the family in mat-ters of teen-age sexuality has declined while "the peer group and peer culture are becoming more important,"[3] the ninth-graders were still sensitive to parental fears.

Sex

"Are there pressures on you [from peers] to have sex?" "Some," said Elaine, "but I'm old enough to handle it." The other girls said that they, too, had had sexual advances made to them but, as Donna explained, "a guy wouldn't want to make a girl he likes mad at him by trying to do something she didn't want him to do. If a girl tells a boy to stop, he'll stop if he really likes her. If he doesn't stop then he has to be mentally ill and I wouldn't want to go out with a guy who is mentally ill."

The interviewer continued to explore their attitudes toward teenage relations with opposite-sex peers and sexual activity. "If a girl can control a boy's behavior then why do some girls have sex with boys? Do you think they are trying to win popularity with boys by having sex with them?" she asked. "Lots of girls try to be popular that way," they said. This response from both the boys and girls was followed by Jeffrey's comment, "Boys don't really like girls who have sex with them. Most of the boys who date girls who have sex with them tell other guys about them. They say we should go out with them, too, because, 'she'll do this and she'll do that.' " "A lot of guys are just out for good looks and thrills [sex]," commented Jonathan. "They go with a girl for a few months and then they deliberately break up with her. Sometimes when they see those girls in the halls at school they won't even speak to them."

Paul spoke with regret and sympathy for two girls he knew who had become pregnant during the previous school year. "Lori Ann had an abortion during the summer and now she's back in school. I don't know the boy who made her pregnant but he doesn't have anything to worry about. It ruined Lori Ann," he said. "Some boys think it is OK to have sex with girls because they know nothing will happen to them if the girl gets pregnant," said Jeffrey. "The most that will happen to him is that he will feel guilty. Maybe the girl's family will kill him but the girl has to live with the problem."

The boys' description of the exploitation of girls by male peers enraged the girls. "If a guy goes around with girls because they'll have sex with him then he's on some kind of ego trip and wants to prove something," said Elizabeth. "It's no good dating that kind of guy. Maybe when he matures enough he will be able to understand what a girl wants out of a relationship instead of thinking only about what he wants. Maybe he will be able to see a girl for what she is instead of for what she does when she goes out on a date with him."

Laura agreed. "Having sex with a boy is not a whole relationship. Kids in junior high school aren't in love. Nobody can know what love with a person of the opposite-sex is until they are mature. Having sex with a boy our age might make two people feel closer together at the time but not later." "That's right," said Elaine. "Love is something deeper and more mature than the feelings we have for the guys right now. When a girl is really mature and loves a guy she'd probably want to have sex with him and she wouldn't care what anyone thought. But at our age we only like, not love, the boys we go around with. We don't love them like a husband we are going to spend the rest of our lives with."

There were other kinds of problems. "It seems to me," said Elizabeth, "that girls have more problems among themselves when they are dating guys. Take Maureen, for example. She doesn't do anything [have sex] with boys but a lot of guys want to go steady with her because she is so pretty. That makes other girls jealous and they say mean things about her. They tell other kids that she does things [has sex] with guys when she doesn't."

And there were problems with relations between the sexes. "Some guys, you know, get jealous if they just see a girl they like talking to another boy. That makes the girl feel she can't even be a friend to that boy even though they've been good friends for years. Going steady limits a person. Sometimes it's not worth it," said Elaine. Donna agreed. "Boyfriends expect more of a girl than a boy who is just a friend. Sometimes I think it is more fun to be just friends with everyone. I know I have more fun when I'm not dating."

The boys admitted that they felt the same restraints as girls. "Once I went steady with a girl and when we broke up she wouldn't be friends with me ever again. She doesn't even like me anymore. She won't speak to me in the halls at school even when I try to speak to her. She is really mad at me," said Jonathan. "Why do you think that happens?" asked the interviewer. "It seems to me," said Laura, "that when a girl becomes a girlfriend to a boy they get really close and they get to know one another real well. Then when they break up it takes a long time to get over being girlfriend and boyfriend. They have to get over that relationship before they can be just friends again." "Then why do you have dating relationships?" asked the interviewer. "Because it's worth it. Everybody has a girlfriend or a boyfriend," said Donna.

Vocabulary

The interviewer ended the session by asking if the ninth-graders remembered their elementary school years and if the experiences that I had given them had any value in their present lives. "You spent a lot of time with Ms. Best when you were in elementary school. Do you think you're any different from your friends who didn't spend all that time with her?" the interviewer asked. "We're not different," said Donna, "but we talked more about love and friendship and sex than other kids did. It seems to me that because we had more experience talking with one another at that age we can be more open with other people now. She made us feel close to one another so that we could talk openly about anything that was important to us."

"Our whole class felt like one big group and we did everything together," said Elaine. "We had a fun time and, I suppose, we felt special. Now it is easy for us to be open with people even when we meet them for the first time. We're not embarrassed to talk about things like love and sex because we talked about those things a lot in elementary school."

Paul agreed. "When we were in sixth grade and we all got together we could talk about whatever we wanted to talk about. That helped prepare the way for us in junior high school. When we got here we all knew that we had some really good friends we could talk to if we ever needed someone. And we can still talk about anything. Ms. Best let us have experiences others kids never get."

"What do you think, Jonathan? Did it make a difference to you to be in a group that could express feelings?" asked the interviewer. "It most certainly did," he replied. "Our group was a lot more open about things that are important to us than most people I know. More open than a lot of my friends in junior high school." Then Jonathan turned to the president of the student council and asked, "Don't you agree that the kids in our class who came from Pine Hill are a lot more open about things than the other kids at our school?" "Yes, I do," he replied. "It seems easier for you to express feelings than for the rest of us."

The "things" of which they spoke were the feelings they had about their own bodies, about love and sex, about liking and friendship between opposite-sex peers. The scanty knowledge acquired from a variety of sex games had ill equipped them to know the difference between sex and love and friendship and liking. Nor was there any way they would learn about relationships between the sexes while they organized their separate worlds around the rules of the second curriculum. Had they carried their ignorance with them into junior high school, they might have "experimented" with sex to learn more, for it is from peers, not parents or teachers, that teenagers receive their information both about sexual relations and about appropriate gender-role relationships between the sexes.

Further reassuring discussions with the ninth-grade boys and girls showed that there had not, in fact, been a permanent concession to the peer culture in grade seven. They explained their behavior at that time as a response to being low man on the totem pole.

The Pine Hill boys and girls had brought into a new environment a set of attitudes and behavior unfamiliar to its inhabitants. This made them subject to misunderstanding, not to mention taunting, from the older students. When they became ninth-graders and were in a position to modify the structure of the peer culture, to be the imitated rather than the imitators, they could once more be themselves. Donna succinctly explained the penalties of being the youngest students in the school and the privileges that accrue to the oldest. "When we were in seventh grade we felt like nobodies. The older kids were always telling us we were little babies who didn't know anything. Well, we're in ninth grade now and we can do what we want to do and they [the seventh- and eighth-graders] can't say or do anything about it. Now *they* are afraid of us." And, it turned out, when they could do and say what they wanted, they were indeed egalitarian, they were indeed nonsexist, they could indeed relate to one another on the basis of common interests—as friends—without resorting to macho aggression or female wiles. But, they told the NOVA interviewer, it was not always easy.

Notes

Introduction

1. Susan Brainard Gage, ed., *Learning Disabilities: Issues and Recommendations for Research*, papers derived from the National Institute of Education Conference on Learning Disabilities, July 1947 (Washington: NIE, 1975), p. 3.
2. Willard W. Hartup, "The Origins of Friendship," in *Friendship and Peer Relations*, ed. Michael Lewis and Leonard Rosenblum (New York: Wiley, 1975), p. 3.
3. Lewis and Rosenblum, Introduction to *Friendship and Peer Relations*, p. 6.

Chapter 1: Formation of Groups

1. Eleanor Maccoby and Carol Jacklin, *The Psychology of Sex Differences* (Stanford: Stanford University Press, 1974), pp. 226–27.

Chapter 2: The Tent Club

1. M. R. Feinberg, M. Smith, and R. Schmidt, "An Analysis of Expressions Used by Adolescents of Varying Economic Levels to Describe Accepted and Rejected Peers," *Journal of Genetic Psychology* 93 (1958): 133–48.

Chapter 3: Winners and Losers

1. Lionel Tiger notes an analogous antifamily emphasis in his discussion of secret societies: "Indeed the male bonding process, for which in these circumstances initiations are so important, may constitute a strong inducement to sever family-of-origin ties and to circumscribe reproductive family activity. An initiation ceremony may symbolize the actual break. . . . A similar anti-family bond for adults is not uncommon" (Lionel Tiger, *Men In Groups* [New York: Random House, 1969], p. 135).

Chapter 4: Some Consequences of Rejection

1. George D. Spache, "Contributions of Allied Fields to the Teaching of Reading," in *Innovation and Change in Reading Instruction*, The Sixty-Seventh Yearbook of the National Society for the Study of Education (Chicago: University of Chicago Press, 1968), pp. 248–49. Emphasis added.
2. Sarane Spence Boocock, *An Introduction to the Sociology of Learning* (Boston: Houghton Mifflin, 1972), p. 207.
3. David C. Epperson, "Some Interpersonal and Performance Correlates of Classroom Alienation," *The School Review* (Autumn 1963): 374.
4. Ibid., p. 361.
5. Steven R. Asher, Sherri L. Oden, and John M. Gottman, "Children's Friendships in School Settings," *Early Childhood Education* (Fall 1975): 19.
6. *The Washington Post*, April 11, 1978, Metro, p. 1.

179

Chapter 5: What Was Being Taught

1. *300 Names for Baby* (New York: Dell, 1969).
2. Whitney Darrow, Jr., *I'm Glad I'm a Boy! I'm Glad I'm a Girl!* (New York: Simon and Schuster, 1970), unnumbered pages.
3. Beeman N. Phillips and M. Vere DeVault, *Psychology* (Austin: The Steck Company, 1959), pp. 12–13.
4. Darrow, *I'm Glad I'm a Boy!*
5. D. Walley, *What Little Boys Can Be* (Kansas City: Hallmark, Little Golden Books, n.d.).
6. D. Walley, *What Little Girls Can Be* (Kansas City: Hallmark, Little Golden Books, n.d.).
7. Bill Martin, Jr. (adapted by), *Whistle, Mary, Whistle* (New York: Holt, Rinehart and Winston, 1970).
8. *A Duck Is a Duck* (Third Primer) (Lexington, Mass.: Ginn & Company, 1964).
9. *May I Come In?* (First Reader) (Lexington, Mass.: Ginn & Company, 1964).

Chapter 6: What Was Being Learned: The Boys

1. A. E. Lindgren, *Pippi Longstocking* (New York: Viking, 1950).
2. In March 1975 a reporter from the *Washington Post* visited Buckingham Elementary School in Prince Georges County, Maryland, and found the children in the first grade playing similar games. "Another thing . . . very big is 'frontsies.' This is when somebody lets you get in front of them in line. It's sort of a 'no-no' because when you let somebody in front of you, then the people behind you are pushed further back. 'Buttsies' is when you cut into line. A reporter observed that 'buttsies' can quickly lead to what can only be termed 'punchies.' Being first in line is like the most important thing." *The Washington Post*, March 31, 1975, *The Maryland Weekly*, p. 1.
3. Warren Farrell, *The Liberated Man* (New York: Random House, 1974), p. 30.
4. Rudyard Kipling, "If," in *One Thousand Poems for Children*, selected by Elizabeth Sechrist (Turbotville, Tenn.: Macrae-Smith Company, 1946).
5. John Greenleaf Whittier, "In School Days," in Sechrist, *One Thousand Poems*.
6. Howard S. Becker, *Outsiders: Studies in the Sociology of Deviance* (New York: The Free Press, 1973), p. 1.

Chapter 7: What Was Being Learned: The Girls

1. Eleanor Maccoby and Carol Jacklin, *The Psychology of Sex Differences* (Stanford: Stanford University Press, 1974), p. 223.
2. Ibid.
3. Ibid., p. 222.
4. Webster's International Dictionary defines gynandry as "intersexuality."

Chapter 9: Games of Chance

1. Richard Cohen, "Dubious Achievement for All Concerned," *Washington Post*, January 23, 1979, Metro, p. 1.

Chapter 10: Clearing the Debris

1. Ruth Hartley, "Sex-Role Pressures in the Socialization of the Male Child," *Psychological Reports* 5 (1959): 457–68.
2. Carol Ryrie Brink, *Caddie Woodlawn* (New York: Macmillan, 1935), p. 13.
3. Ibid., pp. 239–40.
4. Dodie Smith, *One Hundred and One Dalmations* (New York: Viking, 1957).

Chapter 11: Fading Stereotypes

1. *Washington Post*, May 23, 1976, p. B 3.
2. "No, No, Rosina," in *The Dog Next Door* (Lexington, Mass.: Ginn & Company, 1964), pp. 216–24.

Chapter 12: It Could Be Done

1. The changes in the boys' attitudes toward machismo also made it possible for those boys excluded from peer-group activity in the third grade to find acceptance in the sixth grade.
2. Title IX, an implementing regulation of the Educational Amendments of 1972, states: "No person in the United States shall, on the basis of sex, be excluded from participation in, be denied the benefits of, or be subjected to discrimination under any educational program or activity receiving Federal financial assistance."

Epilogue

1. NBC Evening News, "Sex Roles, Segment 3," Mary Ann Maskery, commentator, June 1977 and January 1978.
2. The adult attitudes that hampered girls who had athletic ability equal to or better than that of boys harked back to the Victorian era and the beginning of team sports. Sabo and Runfola say of this era, "There, of course, remained the strong suspicion in those times that any unnecessary contact between the sexes was bound to lead to damnation. To have been playing sports together might well bring down the Empire." (Donald Sebo and Ross Runfola, *Jock: Sports and Male Identity* [Englewood Cliffs, N.J.: Prentice-Hall, 1980], p. 11.) Perhaps the teachers who so rigorously opposed permitting boys and girls to play in the same sports events thought that such indiscretion might well bring down the Junior High School.
3. The University of West Florida, *Laving the Groundwork for an Interdisciplinary Effort Aimed at Prevention of Pregnancy among Middle School Youth*, final report (Pensacola: University of West Florida, July 1, 1978–June 30, 1979), p. 4.